WITH FULL PURPOSE OF HEART

MESSAGES BY
DALLIN H. OAKS

**DESERET
BOOK**

SALT LAKE CITY, UTAH

Library of Congress Cataloging-in-Publication Data

Oaks, Dallin H.
  With full purpose of heart / Dallin H. Oaks.
      p.   cm.
  Includes bibliographical references and index.
  ISBN 1-57008-934-5 (alk. paper)
    1. Church of Jesus Christ of Latter-day Saints—Doctrines.   2. Mormon Church—Doctrines.   3. Christian life—Moromon authors.   I. Title.
  BX8635.3 O24   2002
  230'.9332—dc21   2002010914

Printed in the United States of America   72076-7019
Publishers Printing, Salt Lake City, Utah

10   9   8   7   6   5   4   3   2   1

CONTENTS

Contents

PREFACE

THIS IS A BOOK ABOUT THE LORD Jesus Christ and the plan of salvation. There is nothing new here. The doctrine and principles are familiar. But when any soul gains an increased understanding of an eternal truth, that is something significant. And if increased understanding can help a soul keep the commandments of God "with full purpose of heart" and live in greater harmony with eternal truth, that is something wonderful for everyone.

The chapters of this book discuss doctrine and principles, and their application to the joys and challenges of life. All were prepared originally as individual messages for audiences of Church members. Almost all have been published earlier, from 1981 to 2002, most in the *Ensign* or in the compilations of speeches given at Brigham Young University. Why publish them again? We hope that bringing them together here will facilitate access and cause the persuasiveness of the compiled whole to be greater than the sum of the scattered parts.

This book is a personal expression and is not an official statement of the doctrine of The Church of Jesus Christ of Latter-day Saints.

ACKNOWLEDGMENTS

I AM GRATEFUL TO SHERI L. DEW, Robert L. Millet, and Cory Maxwell, who persuaded me that this compilation could be valuable. I am also grateful to Michael Morris, who suggested the light editing required to change a talk given to one audience at one time into a chapter of a book published at another time.

1

WHAT THINK YE
OF CHRIST?

WHAT THINK YE OF CHRIST?" (Matthew 22:42). That question is as penetrating today as when Jesus used it to confound the Pharisees almost two thousand years ago. Like a sword, sharp and powerful, it uncovers what is hidden, divides truth from error, and goes to the heart of religious belief. Here are some answers being given today.

Some praise Jesus Christ as the greatest teacher who ever lived but deny that He is the Messiah, Savior, or Redeemer. Some prominent theologians teach that our secularized world needs "a new concept of God," stripped of the supernatural. They believe that not even a suffering God can help solve the pain and tragedy of modern man.[1] A bishop in one Christian denomination has declared that "Jesus was in every sense a human being, just as we are."[2]

Another church that claims roots in Christianity maintains that Jesus' crucifixion was not the fulfillment of His mission but evidence of its failure. They teach that He did not cleanse men of original sin and that another messiah must come to complete our salvation and establish the kingdom of heaven on earth.[3]

Under the influence of such teachings, the religion of many is like the creed of humanists, who declare that "no deity will save us; we must save ourselves."[4]

Many years ago a young Latter-day Saint enrolled in a Midwestern university and applied for a scholarship available only to Christians. Both the applicant and the university officials were unsure whether a Latter-day Saint was eligible. After consulting a panel of theologians, they concluded that this student was a Christian after all.

When I first heard of that event more than thirty years ago, I was shocked that anyone, especially a member of our church, would entertain any doubt that we are Christians. I have come to a better understanding of that confusion. I think we sometimes thoughtlessly give others cause to wonder. How does this happen?

For many years I was a teacher of law. A frequent teaching method in that discipline is to concentrate classroom instruction on the difficult questions—the obscure and debatable matters that lie at the fringes of learning. Some law teachers believe that the simple general rules that answer most legal questions are so obvious that students can learn them by independent study. As a result, these teachers devote little time to teaching the basics.

I believe some of us sometimes do the same thing in gospel teaching. We neglect to teach and testify to some simple, basic truths of paramount importance. This omission permits some members and nonmembers to get wrong ideas about our faith and beliefs.

What do members of The Church of Jesus Christ of Latter-day Saints think of Christ? We believe that Jesus Christ is the Only Begotten Son of God the Eternal Father. He is our Creator. He is our Teacher. He is our Savior. His atonement paid for the sin of Adam and won victory over death, assuring resurrection and immortality for all men.

He is all of these, but He is more. Jesus Christ is the Savior, whose atoning sacrifice opens the door for us to be cleansed of our personal sins so that we can be readmitted into the presence of God. He is our Redeemer.

The Messiah's atoning sacrifice is the central message of the prophets of all ages. It was prefigured by the animal sacrifices prescribed by the law of Moses, whose whole meaning, one prophet explained, "point[ed] to that great and last sacrifice [of] . . . the Son of God, yea, infinite and eternal" (Alma 34:14). The Atonement was promised and predicted by the Old Testament prophets. Isaiah declared:

"He was wounded for our transgressions, he was bruised for our iniquities . . . and with his stripes we are healed.

"All we like sheep have gone astray; we have turned every one to his own way; and the Lord hath laid on him the iniquity of us all.

"He was . . . brought as a lamb to the slaughter. . . . He was cut off out of the land of the living: for the transgression of my people was he stricken. . . .

"He bare the sin of many, and made intercession for the transgressors" (Isaiah 53:5–8, 12).

At the beginning of the Savior's ministry, John the Baptist exclaimed, "Behold the Lamb of God, which taketh away the sin of the world" (John 1:29). At the end of the Savior's ministry, as Jesus blessed the cup and gave it to His disciples, He said, "This is my blood of the new testament, which is shed for many for the remission of sins" (Matthew 26:28). As we partake of the sacrament of the Lord's Supper, we drink in "remembrance of [His] blood . . . which was shed for [us]" (D&C 20:79).

The writers of the New Testament taught that our Savior's suffering and blood atoned for our sins. The Apostle Paul told the Corinthians that the first principle of the gospel he preached to them was "how that Christ died for our sins according to the scriptures" (1 Corinthians 15:3). And to the Colossians he wrote, "We have redemption through his blood, even the forgiveness of sins" (Colossians 1:14; Hebrews 2:17; 10:10).

Peter described how Christ "bare our sins in his own body on the tree, that we, being dead to sins, should live unto righteousness: by whose stripes ye were healed" (1 Peter 2:24).

John wrote that "the blood of Jesus Christ . . . cleanseth us from all sin" (1 John 1:7; 2:2; 3:5; 4:10).

We revere the Bible. And so, we and our fellow believers in Christ sing these words from that inspiring hymn "How Great Thou Art":

> And when I think that God, his Son not sparing,
> Sent him to die, I scarce can take it in,
> That on the cross my burden gladly bearing
> He bled and died to take away my sin.[5]

Although the Bible's explanation of atonement for individual sins should be unmistakable, that doctrine has been misunderstood by many who have only the Bible to explain it. Modern prophets declare that the Book of Mormon contains the fulness of the everlasting gospel in greater clarity than any other scripture (D&C 20:8–9; 27:5). In a day when many are challenging the divinity of Jesus Christ or doubting the reality of His atonement and resurrection, the message of that second witness, the Book of Mormon, is needed more urgently than ever.

President Ezra Taft Benson reminded us again and again that the Book of Mormon "was written for our day" and that it "is the keystone in our witness of Jesus Christ."[6] I believe that our Heavenly Father has had His prophets direct us into a more intensive study of the Book of Mormon because this generation needs its message more than any of its forebears. As President Benson said, the Book of Mormon "provides the most complete explanation of the doctrine of the Atonement," and "its testimony of the Master is clear, undiluted, and full of power."[7]

In contrast, what is called "liberal theology" teaches that Jesus Christ is important not because He atoned for our sins but because He taught us the way to come to God by perfecting ourselves. In this theology, human beings can be reconciled to God entirely through their own righteousness.[8] Another group—secular rather than religious—believes that Jesus was not God, that man is God, and that we can create our own destiny through the powers of our own mind.[9]

Are Latter-day Saints susceptible to such heresies? The Apostle Paul wrote that we should "work out [our] own salvation with fear and trembling" (Philippians 2:12). Could that familiar expression mean that the sum total of our own righteousness will win us salvation and exaltation? Could some of us believe that our heavenly parentage and our divine destiny allow us to pass through mortality and attain eternal life solely on our own merits?

On the basis of what I have heard, I believe that some of us, some of the time, say things that can create that impression. We can forget that keeping the commandments, which is necessary, is not sufficient. As Nephi said, we must labor diligently to persuade everyone "to believe in Christ, and to be reconciled to God; for we know that it is by grace that we are saved, after all we can do" (2 Nephi 25:23).

In his famous poem "Invictus," William Ernest Henley hurled man's challenge against fate. With head "bloody, but unbowed," determined man is unconquerable. The last verse reads:

> It matters not how strait the gate,
> How charged with punishments the scroll,
> I am the master of my fate.
> I am the captain of my soul.[10]

Writing a half-century later, Elder Orson F. Whitney replied with these lines:

Art thou in truth? Then what of him
Who bought thee with his blood?
Who plunged into devouring seas
And snatched thee from the flood?

Who bore for all our fallen race
What none but him could bear.—
The God who died that man might live,
And endless glory share?

Of what avail thy vaunted strength,
Apart from his vast might?
Pray that his Light may pierce the gloom,
That thou mayest see aright.

Men are as bubbles on the wave,
As leaves upon the tree.
Thou, captain of thy soul, forsooth!
Who gave that place to thee?

Free will is thine—free agency,
To wield for right or wrong;
But thou must answer unto him
To whom all souls belong.

Bend to the dust that head "unbowed,"
Small part of Life's great whole!
And see in him, and him alone,
The Captain of thy soul.[11]

Man unquestionably has impressive powers and can bring to pass great things by tireless efforts and indomitable will. But after all our obedience and good works, we cannot be saved from the effect of our sins without the grace extended by the atonement of Jesus Christ.

The Book of Mormon puts us right. It teaches that "salvation doth not come by the law alone" (Mosiah 13:28); that is, salvation does not come by keeping the commandments alone. "By the law no flesh is justified" (2 Nephi 2:5). Even those who serve

God with their "whole souls" are "unprofitable servants" (Mosiah 2:21). We cannot earn our own salvation.

The Book of Mormon teaches, "Since man had fallen he could not merit anything of himself" (Alma 22:14). "There can be nothing which is short of an infinite atonement which will suffice for the sins of the world" (Alma 34:12; 2 Nephi 9:7; Alma 34:8–16). "Wherefore, redemption cometh in and through the Holy Messiah; . . . he offereth himself a sacrifice for sin, to answer the ends of the law" (2 Nephi 2:6–7).

In the Book of Mormon the Savior explains the gospel, including the Atonement and its relationship to repentance, baptism, works of righteousness, and the ultimate judgment:

"My Father sent me that I might be lifted up upon the cross; . . . that I might draw all men unto me, . . . that they may be judged according to their works. And . . . whoso repenteth and is baptized in my name shall be filled; and if he endureth to the end, behold, him will I hold guiltless before my Father at that day when I shall stand to judge the world" (3 Nephi 27:14–16).

The Savior then restates these principles in a way that emphasizes our everlasting reliance on the Atonement worked out by the shedding of His blood:

"And no unclean thing can enter into [the Father's] kingdom; therefore nothing entereth into his rest save it be those who have washed their garments in my blood, because of their faith, and the repentance of all their sins, and their faithfulness unto the end" (3 Nephi 27:19).

Joseph Smith stated this same relationship in our third article of faith: "We believe that through the Atonement of Christ, all mankind may be saved, by obedience to the laws and ordinances of the Gospel" (Articles of Faith 1:3).

Why is Christ the only way? How was it possible for Him to take upon Himself the sins of all mankind? Why was it necessary for His blood to be shed? And how can our soiled and sinful selves be cleansed by His blood?

These are mysteries I do not understand. To me, as to President John Taylor, the miracle of the atonement of Jesus Christ is "incomprehensible and inexplicable."[12] But the Holy Ghost has given me a witness of its truthfulness, and I rejoice that I can spend my life proclaiming it.

I testify with the ancient and modern prophets that "there is none other name [and no other way] under heaven . . . whereby we must be saved" (Acts 4:12; 2 Nephi 25:20; Alma 38:9; D&C 18:23).

I witness with the prophet Lehi that "there is no flesh that can dwell in the presence of God, save it be through the merits, and mercy, and grace of the Holy Messiah" (2 Nephi 2:8).

I testify with the prophet Alma that no man can be saved except he is "cleansed from all stain, through the blood of [Jesus Christ]" (Alma 5:21). "Repentance," he explained, "could not come unto men except there were a punishment" (Alma 42:16), and "therefore God himself atoneth for the sins of the world, to bring about the plan of mercy, to appease the demands of justice" (Alma 42:15).

I witness with the prophets of the Book of Mormon that the Messiah, the Holy One of Israel, suffered, "according to the flesh" (Alma 7:13), the pains, the infirmities, and the griefs and sorrows of every living creature in the family of Adam (2 Nephi 9:21; Alma 7:12–13; Mosiah 14:4; D&C 18:11).

I testify that when the Savior suffered and died for all God's children, they became subject unto Him (2 Nephi 9:5) and to His commandment that "all must repent and be baptized in his name, having perfect faith in [him] . . . or they cannot be saved in the kingdom of God" (2 Nephi 9:23; Alma 11:40; John 3:5; John 8:24).

Speaking through the Prophet Joseph Smith in our dispensation, the Savior said:

"I am . . . Christ the Lord, . . . the Redeemer of the world. I [have] accomplished and finished the will of him whose I am, even the Father, concerning me—having done this that I might subdue all things unto myself—

"Retaining all power, even to . . . judging every man according to his works and the deeds which he hath done. And surely every man must repent or suffer, for I, God, am endless. . . . Wherefore, I command you to repent. . . .

"For behold, I, God, have suffered these things for all, that they might not suffer if they would repent; but if they would not repent they must suffer even as I" (D&C 19:1–4, 13, 16–17).

What think we of Christ? As members of The Church of Jesus Christ of Latter-day Saints, we testify with the Book of Mormon prophet-king Benjamin that "there shall be no other name given nor any other way nor means whereby salvation can come unto the children of men, only in and through the name of Christ, the Lord Omnipotent. For behold, . . . salvation was, and is, and is to come, in and through the atoning blood of Christ" (Mosiah 3:17–18).

As we repent of our sins and seek to keep His commandments and our covenants, we cry out, as Benjamin's people cried out, "O have mercy, and apply the atoning blood of Christ that we may receive forgiveness of our sins" (Mosiah 4:2).

In all of this, we remember and rely on the Lord's sure word: "Keep my commandments in all things. And, if you keep my commandments and endure to the end you shall have eternal life, which gift is the greatest of all the gifts of God" (D&C 14:6–7).

From an address published in the Ensign, *November 1988, 65–68.*

NOTES

1. John A. Hardon, *Christianity in the Twentieth Century,* Garden City, N.Y.: Doubleday, 1971, 356, 359.
2. "One Clergyman's Views on the 'Death of God,'" *U.S. News & World Report,* 18 April 1966, 57.

3. Holy Spirit Association for the Unification of World Christianity, *Outline of the Principle, Level 4,* 1980, 79–83, 238–39, 247–48, 252, 298–99.

4. *The Encyclopedia of American Religions: Religious Creeds,* ed. J. Gordon Melton, 1st ed., Detroit: Gale Research, 1973, 641.

5. *Hymns of the Church of Jesus Christ of Latter-day Saints,* Salt Lake City: The Church of Jesus Christ of Latter-day Saints, 1985, no. 86.

6. "The Book of Mormon—Keystone of Our Religion," *Ensign,* November 1986, 5–6.

7. "The Book of Mormon—Keystone of Our Religion," 5.

8. O. Kendall White Jr., *Mormon Neo-Orthodoxy: A Crisis Theology,* Salt Lake City: Signature Books, 1987, 43–44.

9. Derk Kinnane Roelofsma, "Age-old Fear of New Age Concerns," *Insight,* 11 July 1988, 54.

10. *Out of the Best Books,* ed. Bruce B. Clark and Robert K. Thomas, 5 vols., Salt Lake City: Deseret Book, 1968, 4:93.

11. "The Soul's Captain," *Improvement Era,* May 1926, 611.

12. *The Mediation and Atonement of Our Lord and Savior Jesus Christ,* Salt Lake City: Deseret News, 1882, 148–49.

2

THE LIGHT AND LIFE
OF THE WORLD

THE BOOK OF MORMON TELLS of the resurrected Lord visiting some of the people of the Americas. Clothed in a white robe, He descended out of heaven. Standing in the midst of a multitude, He stretched forth His hand and said:

"Behold, I am Jesus Christ, whom the prophets testified shall come into the world. And behold, I am the light and the life of the world" (3 Nephi 11:10–11).

He has repeated this declaration in many modern revelations (D&C 12:9, 39:2, 45:7). In harmony with His words, we solemnly affirm that Jesus Christ, the Only Begotten Son of God the Eternal Father, is the light and life of the world.

Jesus Christ is the light and life of the world because all things were made by Him. Under the direction and according to the plan of God the Father, Jesus Christ is the Creator, the source of the light and life of all things.

Through modern revelation we have the testimony of John,

who bore record that Jesus Christ is "the light and the Redeemer of the world; the Spirit of truth, who came into the world, because the world was made by him, and in him was the life of men and the light of men. The worlds were made by him; men were made by him; all things were made by him, and through him, and of him" (D&C 93:9–10).

Jesus Christ is the *light* of the world because He is the source of the light that "proceedeth forth from the presence of God to fill the immensity of space" (D&C 88:12). His light is "the true light that lighteth every man that cometh into the world" (D&C 93:2; D&C 84:46). The scriptures call this universal light "the light of truth" (D&C 88:6), "the light of Christ" (D&C 88:7; Moroni 7:18), and the "Spirit of Christ" (Moroni 7:16). This is the light that quickens our understanding (D&C 88:11). It is "the light by which [we] may judge" (Moroni 7:18). It "is given to every man, that he may know good from evil" (Moroni 7:16).

Jesus Christ is also the light of the world because His example and His teachings illuminate the path we should walk to return to the presence of our Father in Heaven. Before Jesus was born, Zacharias prophesied that the Lord God of Israel would visit His people "to give light to them that sit in darkness and in the shadow of death, to guide [their] feet into the way of peace" (Luke 1:79).

During His ministry in the Americas, Jesus taught, "Behold I am the light; I have set an example for you" (3 Nephi 18:16). Later, He told His apostles, "Hold up your light that it may shine unto the world," adding, "Behold, I am the light which ye shall hold up—that which ye have seen me do" (3 Nephi 18:24). He taught the Nephite multitude, "Ye know the things that ye must do in my church; for the works which ye have seen me do that shall ye also do" (3 Nephi 27:21).

The Savior emphasized the close relationship between His light and His commandments when He taught the Nephites, "Behold, I am the law, and the light" (3 Nephi 15:9). The

Psalmist expressed that relationship: "Thy word is a lamp unto my feet, and a light unto my path" (Psalm 119:105).

As the Lord led Lehi and his people out of Jerusalem, He said, "I will also be your light in the wilderness; and I will prepare the way before you, if it so be that ye shall keep my commandments" (1 Nephi 17:13).

As we keep the Lord's commandments, we see His light ever brighter on our path and we realize the fulfillment of Isaiah's promise: "And the Lord shall guide thee continually" (Isaiah 58:11).

Jesus Christ is also the light of the world because His power persuades us to do good. The prophet Mormon taught, "All things which are good cometh of God. . . . Wherefore, every thing which inviteth and enticeth to do good, and to love God, and to serve him, is inspired of God" (Moroni 7:12–13).

Mormon's words anticipate what the Lord later told Moroni while he was compiling the Book of Mormon: "He that believeth these things which I have spoken . . . shall know that these things are true; for it persuadeth men to do good. And whatsoever thing persuadeth men to do good is of me; for good cometh of none save it be of me. . . . I am the light, and the life, and the truth of the world" (Ether 4:11–12; D&C 11:12).

And so we see that Jesus Christ is the *light* of the world because He is the source of the light that quickens our understanding, because His teachings and His example illuminate our path, and because His power persuades us to do good.

Jesus Christ is the *life* of the world because of His unique position in what the scriptures call "the great and eternal plan of deliverance from death" (2 Nephi 11:5).

Jesus taught, "I am the door: by me if any man enter in, he shall be saved. . . . I am come that they might have life, and that they might have it more abundantly" (John 10:9–10).

Later, Jesus explained to His apostles, "I am the way, the

truth, and the life: no man cometh unto the Father, but by me" (John 14:6).

We come to the Father through the life-giving mission of the Son in two ways. In each of these ways, Jesus Christ is the life of the world, our Savior and our Redeemer.

Through the power and example of the infinite atonement of Jesus Christ, all mankind will be resurrected (2 Nephi 9:7, 12). Our mortal life came into being because of His creative act. Our immortal life has now been assured because the resurrected Lord has redeemed us from death. According to the plan of the Father, the Son was "the firstborn from the dead" (Colossians 1:18). "As in Adam all die, even so in Christ shall all be made alive" (1 Corinthians 15:22).

Jesus Christ is also the life of the world because He has atoned for the sins of the world. By yielding to temptation, Adam and Eve were "cut off from the presence of the Lord" (Helaman 14:16). In the scriptures, this separation is called spiritual death (Helaman 14:16; D&C 29:41).

The atonement of our Savior overcame this spiritual death. The scriptures say, "The Son of God hath atoned for original guilt" (Moses 6:54). As Paul taught the Saints in Rome, "Therefore as by the offence of one judgment came upon all men to condemnation; even so by the righteousness of one the free gift came upon all men unto justification of life" (Romans 5:18). As a result of this atonement, "men will be punished for their own sins, and not for Adam's transgression" (Articles of Faith 1:2).

Our Savior has redeemed us from the sin of Adam, but what about the effects of our own sins? Since "all have sinned" (Romans 3:23), we are all spiritually dead. Again, our only hope for life is our Savior, who, the prophet Lehi taught, "offereth himself a sacrifice for sin, to answer the ends of the law" (2 Nephi 2:7).

In order to lay claim upon our Savior's life-giving triumph over the spiritual death we suffer because of our own sins, we must follow the conditions He has prescribed. As He has told us in modern revelation, "I, God, have suffered these things for all, that they might not suffer if they would repent; but if they would not repent they must suffer even as I" (D&C 19:16–17).

Our third article of faith describes the Savior's conditions in these words: "We believe that through the Atonement of Christ, all mankind may be saved, by obedience to the laws and ordinances of the Gospel."

In the words of our Savior, recorded in the Book of Mormon as He taught the people in the Americas, "And whosoever will hearken unto my words and repenteth and is baptized, the same shall be saved" (3 Nephi 23:5).

In summary, the Lord Jesus Christ, our Savior and our Redeemer, is the *life* of the world because His resurrection and His atonement save us from both physical and spiritual death. Jacob rejoiced in this gift of life: "O how great the goodness of our God, who prepareth a way for our escape from the grasp of this awful monster; yea, that monster, death and hell, which I call the death of the body, and also the death of the spirit" (2 Nephi 9:10).

I wish that everyone could understand our belief and hear our testimony that Jesus Christ, our Savior and our Redeemer, is the light and life of the world.

Some who profess to be followers of Christ insist that members of The Church of Jesus Christ of Latter-day Saints are not Christians. Indeed, there are those who make their living attacking our church and its doctrines. I wish all of them could have the experience I shared recently.

A friend who was making his first visit to Salt Lake City called on me in my office. He is a well-educated man and a devout and sincere Christian. Although we have not discussed it with each other, we both know that some leaders of his denomination have taught that members of our church are not Christians.

After a short discussion on a matter of common interest, I

told my friend I had something I would like him to see. We walked to Temple Square and into the North Visitors Center, where we viewed pictures of Bible and Book of Mormon apostles and prophets. Then we turned our steps up the inclined walkway to the second level. Here, Thorvaldsen's great statue of the risen Christ dominates a setting suggestive of the immensity of space and the grandeur of the creations of God.

As we emerged and beheld this majestic replica of the *Christus,* arms outstretched and hands showing the wounds of the crucifixion, my friend drew a sharp breath. We stood quietly for a few minutes, enjoying a reverent communion of worshipful thoughts about our Savior. Then, without further conversation, we made our way down to the street level. On the way we walked past the small diorama showing the Prophet Joseph Smith kneeling in the Sacred Grove.

As we left Temple Square and took our leave of one another, my friend took me by the hand. "Thank-you for showing me that," he said. "Now I understand something about your faith that I have never understood before." I hope that every person who has ever had doubts about whether we are Christians can achieve that same understanding.

We love the Lord Jesus Christ. He is the Messiah, our Savior and our Redeemer. His is the only name by which we can be saved (Mosiah 3:17; 5:8; D&C 18:23). We seek to serve Him. We belong to His church, The Church of Jesus Christ of Latter-day Saints. Our missionaries and members testify of Jesus Christ in many nations of the world. As the prophet Nephi wrote in the Book of Mormon, "We talk of Christ, we rejoice in Christ, we preach of Christ, we prophesy of Christ, and we write according to our prophecies, that our children may know to what source they may look for a remission of their sins" (2 Nephi 25:26).

As we state in our first article of faith, "We believe in God, the Eternal Father, and in His Son, Jesus Christ, and in the Holy Ghost." God the Father, the great Elohim, the Almighty God, is the Father of our spirits, the framer of heaven and earth, and the author of the plan of our salvation (Moses 1:31–33; 2:1–2; D&C 20:17–21). Jesus Christ is His Only Begotten Son, Jehovah, the Holy One and God of Israel, the Messiah, "the God of the whole earth" (3 Nephi 11:14). As the Book of Mormon declares, "Salvation was, and is, and is to come, in and through the atoning blood of Christ, the Lord Omnipotent" (Mosiah 3:18; Moses 6:52, 59). The scriptures proclaim and we reverently affirm that Jesus Christ is the light and life of the world.

What does this knowledge mean to Latter-day Saints, who have sought to make their lives holy by entering into covenants to follow Christ? We should live so that we can be enlightened by our Savior's spirit and so that we may hear and heed the ratifying seal of the Holy Ghost, which testifies of the Father and the Son (D&C 20:26). We should study the principles of His gospel and receive its ordinances. We should keep the commandments, including the Savior's two great commandments to love God and to love and serve our neighbor (Matthew 22:36–40). We should be faithful to the covenants we have made in the name of Jesus Christ.

We should give thanks for Christ's absolute gift of immortality. We should also receive the ordinances and keep the covenants necessary to receive His conditional gift of life eternal, "the greatest of all the gifts of God" (D&C 14:7).

In short, Latter-day Saints invite each other and all men and women everywhere to come unto Christ. As a prophet has told us in the Book of Mormon, "I would that ye should come unto Christ, who is the Holy One of Israel, and partake of his salvation, and the power of his redemption. Yea, come unto him, and offer your whole souls as an offering unto him, and continue in fasting and praying, and endure to the end; and as the Lord liveth ye will be saved" (Omni 1:26).

May God bless all of us to come unto Christ.

From an address published in the Ensign, *November 1987, 63–66.*

3

WITNESSES OF CHRIST

I RECEIVED A LETTER FROM A CHURCH member who posed an unusual question: "Do I have a right to bear testimony of the Savior? Or is that the sole prerogative of the Twelve?" In response, I share some thoughts on why every member of this Church should bear witness and testimony of Jesus Christ.

In the beginning, God commanded Adam, "Thou shalt do all that thou doest in the name of the Son, and thou shalt repent and call upon God in the name of the Son forevermore" (Moses 5:8). Then the Holy Ghost, "which beareth record of the Father and the Son," came upon Adam and Eve, and they "blessed the name of God, and they made all things known unto their sons and their daughters" (Moses 5:9, 12).

Later, Enoch described how God had taught Adam that all people must repent and be baptized in the name of Jesus Christ, whose atoning sacrifice made possible the forgiveness of sins, and that they must teach these things to their children (Moses

6:52–59). And so our first parents established the pattern, receiving a testimony from the Holy Ghost and then bearing witness of the Father and the Son to those around them.

We witness of Christ by our membership in the Church that bears His name (3 Nephi 27:7; D&C 115:4). The prophet Nephi described the ordinance of baptism into the Church as an occasion when we witness unto the Father that we are willing to take upon us the name of Christ (2 Nephi 31:13). Similarly, the Lord has specified that those who desire to be baptized in this dispensation should "come forth with broken hearts and contrite spirits, and witness before the church that they . . . are willing to take upon them the name of Jesus Christ" (D&C 20:37; Moroni 6:3). We renew that promise when we partake of the sacrament (D&C 20:77; Moroni 4:3).

We are commanded to pray unto the Father in the name of His Son, Jesus Christ (3 Nephi 18:19, 21, 23; Moses 5:8), and to do "all things . . . in the name of Christ" (D&C 46:31). If we follow these commandments, we serve as witnesses of Jesus Christ through our baptism, our membership in His Church, our partaking of the sacrament, and our prayers and other actions in His name.

But our duty to be witnesses of Jesus Christ requires more than this, and I fear that some of us fall short. We Latter-day Saints can become so preoccupied with our own agendas that we can forget to witness and testify of Christ.

A Church member in the United States described to me in a letter what he had heard in a fast and testimony meeting:

"I sat and listened to seventeen testimonies and never heard Jesus mentioned or referred to in any way. I thought I might be in [some other denomination], but I supposed not because there were no references to God, either. . . .

"The following Sunday, I again attended church. I sat through a priesthood lesson, a gospel doctrine lesson, and seven sacrament meeting speakers and never once heard the name of Jesus or any reference to him."

Perhaps that description is exaggerated. Surely, it is exceptional. I quote it because it provides a vivid reminder for all of us.

In answer to the question, "What are the fundamental principles of your religion?" the Prophet Joseph Smith said, "The fundamental principles of our religion are the testimony of the Apostles and Prophets, concerning Jesus Christ, that He died, was buried, and rose again the third day, and ascended into heaven; and all other things which pertain to our religion are only appendages to it."[1]

When Alma spoke to a group of prospective members at the waters of Mormon, he instructed them on the duties of those who were "desirous to come into the fold of God, and to be called his people" (Mosiah 18:8). One of those duties was "to stand as witnesses of God at all times and in all things, and in all places that ye may be in, even until death" (Mosiah 18:9).

How do members become witnesses beyond the mere fact of their membership? The original apostles were eyewitnesses to the ministry and resurrection of the Savior (Acts 10:39–41). He told them, "Ye shall be witnesses unto me both in Jerusalem, and in all Judaea, and in Samaria, and unto the uttermost part of the earth" (Acts 1:8; Acts 10:42–43). However, He cautioned them that their witnessing would occur after they had received the Holy Ghost (Acts 1:8; Luke 24:49).

An eyewitness was not enough. Even the witness and testimony of the original apostles had to be rooted in the testimony of the Holy Ghost. A prophet has told us that the witness of the Holy Ghost makes an impression on our soul that is more significant than "a visitation of an angel."[2] And the Bible shows that when we testify on the basis of this witness, the Holy Ghost testifies to those who hear our words (Acts 2; 10:44–47).

When the apostles were brought before the civil authorities, Peter testified that Jesus Christ was "a Prince and a Saviour, for to give repentance to Israel, and forgiveness of sins" (Acts 5:31). Then Peter added, "And we are his witnesses of these things; and so is also the Holy Ghost, whom God hath given to them that obey him" (Acts 5:32). The mission of the Holy Ghost is to witness of the Father and the Son (2 Nephi 31:18; 3 Nephi 28:11; D&C 20:27). Consequently, everyone who has received the witness of the Holy Ghost has a duty to share that testimony with others.

Apostles have the calling and ordination to be "special witnesses of the name of Christ in all the world" (D&C 107:23), but the duty to witness and testify of Christ at all times and in all places applies to every member of the Church who has received the testimony of the Holy Ghost.

The book of Luke records two examples of this. In obedience to the law of Moses, Joseph and Mary, after forty days, brought the infant Jesus to the temple at Jerusalem to present Him to the Lord. There, two aged and spiritual temple workers received a witness of His identity and testified of Him. Simeon, who had known by revelation from the Holy Ghost that he should not taste of death until he had seen the Messiah, took the infant in his arms and testified to His divine mission (Luke 2:25–35). Anna, whom the scriptures call "a prophetess" (Luke 2:36), recognized the Messiah "and spake of him to all them that looked for redemption in Jerusalem" (Luke 2:38).

Anna and Simeon were eyewitnesses to the infant, but, just like the apostles, their knowledge of the Savior's divine mission came through the witness of the Holy Ghost. "The testimony of Jesus is the spirit of prophecy" (Revelation 19:10). Therefore, we can properly say that when each received this witness, Simeon was a prophet and Anna was a prophetess. Each then fulfilled the prophetic duty to testify to those around them. As Peter said, "To [Christ] give all the prophets witness" (Acts 10:43). This was what Moses meant when he expressed the wish "that all the Lord's people were prophets, and that the Lord would put his spirit upon them!" (Numbers 11:29).

The scriptures describe other occasions when ordinary men and women bore witness of Christ. The Book of Mormon tells of King Lamoni and his queen, who testified of their Redeemer (Alma 19). The Bible describes the witness of the Holy Ghost coming upon the kinsmen and friends of Cornelius, who were then heard to "magnify God" (Acts 10:24, 46).

Our scriptural duty to witness of the Savior and to testify of His divine Sonship has been affirmed by the prophets in our own day. We are told that the commandments are given and the gospel is proclaimed that every person "might speak in the name of God the Lord, even the Savior of the world" (D&C 1:20).

Spiritual gifts come by the power of the Holy Ghost, that all the faithful may be benefited. One of these gifts is "to know that Jesus Christ is the Son of God, and that he was crucified for the sins of the world" (D&C 46:13). Those who receive this gift have the duty to testify of it. We know this because immediately after describing the gift of knowing that Jesus Christ is the Son of God, the Lord says, "To others it is given to believe on their words, that they also might have eternal life if they continue faithful" (D&C 46:14; 3 Nephi 19:28). Those who have the gift to know must give their witness so that those who have the gift to "believe on their words" can enjoy the benefit of that gift.

Speaking to some of the earliest missionaries of this dispensation, the Lord said: "But with some I am not well pleased, for they will not open their mouths, but they hide the talent which I have given unto them, because of the fear of man. Wo unto such, for mine anger is kindled against them" (D&C 60:2).

In contrast, the Lord gives this great promise to those who are valiant in bearing testimony: "For I will forgive you of your sins with this commandment—that you remain steadfast . . . in bearing testimony to all the world of those things which are communicated unto you" (D&C 84:61). This caution and promise were directed specifically to missionaries, but other scriptures suggest that they apply to other members as well.

In his vision of the spirits of the dead, President Joseph F. Smith described "the spirits of the just" as those "who had been faithful in the testimony of Jesus while they lived in mortality" (D&C 138:12). In contrast, in his vision of the three degrees of glory, the Prophet Joseph Smith described those souls who go to the terrestrial kingdom as the "honorable men of the earth" who were "not valiant in the testimony of Jesus" (D&C 76:75, 79).

What does it mean to be "valiant in the testimony of Jesus"? Surely this includes keeping His commandments and serving Him. But would not it also include bearing witness of Jesus Christ, our Savior and our Redeemer, to believers and non-believers alike? As the Apostle Peter taught the Saints of his day, we should "sanctify the Lord God in [our] hearts: and be ready always to give an answer to every man that asketh [us] a reason of the hope that is in [us]" (1 Peter 3:15).

All of us need to be valiant in the testimony of Jesus. As believers in Christ, we affirm the truth of Peter's testimony in the name of Jesus Christ of Nazareth that "there is none other name under heaven given among men, whereby we must be saved" (Acts 4:12; D&C 109:4). We know from modern revelation that we can come unto the Father only in His name (D&C 93:19). As the Book of Mormon teaches, salvation is "in and through the atoning blood of Christ, the Lord Omnipotent" (Mosiah 3:18; Moses 6:52, 59). To those of us who are devoted to the Lord Jesus Christ, there has never been a greater need for us to profess our faith, privately and publicly.

When the gospel was restored, the pulpits of this land were aflame with the testimony of Jesus, the divine Son of God and Savior of the world. True, the fulness of His doctrine and the power of His priesthood had been lost from the earth, but many good and honorable men and women were valiant in their own testimonies of Jesus. Our earliest missionaries concentrated their message on the Restoration—the calling of the Prophet Joseph Smith and the restoring of priesthood authority—since they could assume that most of those they taught had a fundamental belief in Jesus Christ as their Savior.

Today, our missionaries cannot make that assumption. Many God-fearing people still testify to the divinity of Jesus Christ, but many others—even in the formal ranks of Christianity—doubt His existence or deny His divinity. As I see the deterioration in religious faith that has happened in my own lifetime, I am convinced that we who are members of His Church need to be increasingly valiant in our testimony of Jesus.

Speaking more than thirty years ago, President Harold B. Lee said: "Fifty years ago or more, when I was a missionary, our greatest responsibility was to defend the great truth that the Prophet Joseph Smith was divinely called and inspired and that the Book of Mormon was indeed the word of God. But even at that time there were the unmistakable evidences that there was coming into the religious world actually a question about the Bible and about the divine calling of the Master, himself. Now, fifty years later, our greatest responsibility and anxiety is to defend the divine mission of our Lord and Master, Jesus Christ, for all about us, even among those who claim to be professors of the Christian faith, are those not willing to stand squarely in defense of the great truth that our Lord and Master, Jesus Christ, was indeed the Son of God."[3]

Our knowledge of the literal divinity, resurrection, and atonement of Jesus Christ is more certain and more distinctive with each passing year. That is one reason the Lord has inspired His prophets today to reemphasize our study and testimony of the Book of Mormon, whose mission is "the convincing of the Jew and Gentile that Jesus is the Christ, the Eternal God."[4]

We live in a time when too many who purport to be Christians have a cause that comes ahead of Christ. For example, a national magazine recently reported an innovation by a new bishop of a prominent Christian church. This church's ministers have always consecrated the emblems of the flesh and blood of Jesus Christ in the name of the "Father, Son, and Holy Ghost." However, in an effort to use what are called "nonsexist words," this new bishop has begun to consecrate the emblems in the name of the "Creator, Redeemer, and Sustainer."[5] Such trendy and expedient tampering with the Christian faith illustrates the extent to which some are unwilling to witness of Jesus Christ, the Son of God.

Similar deliberate deviations are not likely to be made by faithful Latter-day Saints. However, we need to be on guard against careless omissions and oversights in our personal testimonies, formal instruction, and worship and funeral services.

In addition, each of us has many opportunities to proclaim our belief to friends and neighbors, fellow workers, and casual acquaintances. I hope we will take these opportunities to express our love for our Savior, our witness of His divine mission, and our determination to serve Him.

If we do all of this, we can say, as the Apostle Paul said, "I am not ashamed of the gospel of Christ: for it is the power of God unto salvation to every one that believeth" (Romans 1:16).

And we can say with the prophet Nephi, "We talk of Christ, we rejoice in Christ, we preach of Christ, we prophesy of Christ, . . . that our children may know to what source they may look for a remission of their sins" (2 Nephi 25:26).

From an address published in the Ensign, *November 1990, 29–32.*

NOTES

1. *Teachings of the Prophet Joseph Smith,* sel. Joseph Fielding Smith, Salt Lake City: Deseret Book, 1976, 121.
2. Joseph Fielding Smith, *Doctrines of Salvation,* comp. Bruce R. McConkie, Salt Lake City: Bookcraft, 1954, 1:44.
3. LDS Student Association fireside address, Utah State University, 10 October 1971.
4. Book of Mormon, title page.
5. "Fretful Murmur in the Cathedral," *Insight,* 24 April 1989, 47.

4

THE GREAT PLAN
OF HAPPINESS

WHERE DID WE COME FROM? Why are we here? Where are we going? Such questions are answered in the gospel of Jesus Christ through what the prophets call the plan of salvation, or "the great plan of happiness" (Alma 42:8). Through inspiration we can understand this road map of eternity and use it to guide our path in mortality.

The gospel teaches us that we are the spirit children of heavenly parents. Before our mortal birth we had "a pre-existent, spiritual personality, as the sons and daughters of the Eternal Father."[1] We were placed here on earth to progress toward our destiny of eternal life. These truths give us a unique perspective and different values to guide our decisions from those who doubt the existence of God and believe that life is the result of random processes.

Our understanding of life begins with a council in heaven. There the spirit children of God were taught His eternal plan for their destiny. We had progressed as far as we could without a physical body and an experience in mortality. To realize a fulness of joy, we had to prove our willingness to keep the commandments of God in a place where we had no memory of what preceded our mortal birth.

In the course of mortality, we would become subject to death, and we would be soiled by sin. To reclaim us from death and sin, our Heavenly Father's plan provided us a Savior whose atonement would redeem all from death and pay the price necessary for all to be cleansed from sin on the conditions He prescribed (2 Nephi 9:19–24).

Satan had his own plan. He proposed to save *all* the spirit children of God, assuring that result by removing their power to choose and thus eliminating the possibility of sin. When Satan's plan was rejected, he and the spirits who followed him opposed the Father's plan and were cast out. All of the myriad mortals who have been born on this earth chose the Father's plan and fought for it. Many of us also made covenants with the Father concerning what we would do in mortality. In ways that have not been revealed, our actions in the spirit world influence us in mortality.

Although Satan and his followers have lost their opportunity to have physical bodies, they are permitted to use their spirit powers to try to frustrate God's plan. Their efforts provide the opposition necessary to test how mortals will use their freedom to choose. Satan's most strenuous opposition is directed at whatever is most important to the Father's plan. Satan seeks to discredit the Savior and divine authority, to nullify the effects of the Atonement, to counterfeit revelation, to lead people away from the truth, to contradict individual accountability, to confuse gender, to undermine marriage, and to discourage childbearing, especially by parents who would raise children in righteousness.

Maleness and femaleness, marriage, and the bearing and nurturing of children are all essential to the great plan of happiness. Modern revelation makes clear that what we call gender was part of our existence prior to our birth. God declares that He created "male and female" (D&C 20:18; Moses 2:27; Genesis 1:27). Elder James E. Talmage explained, "The distinction between male and female is no condition peculiar to the relatively brief period of mortal life; it was an essential characteristic of our pre-existent condition."[2]

To the first man and woman on earth, the Lord said, "Be fruitful, and multiply" (Moses 2:28; Genesis 1:28; Abraham 4:28). This commandment was first in sequence and first in importance. It was essential that God's spirit children have mortal birth and an opportunity to progress toward eternal life. Consequently, all things related to procreation are prime targets for the adversary's efforts to thwart the plan of God.

When Adam and Eve received the first commandment, they were in a transitional state, no longer in the spirit world but with physical bodies not yet subject to death and not yet capable of procreation. They could not fulfill the Father's first command-ment without transgressing the barrier between the bliss of the Garden of Eden and the terrible trials and wonderful opportuni-ties of mortal life.

For reasons that have not been revealed, this transition, or "fall," could not have happened without a transgression—an exer-cise of moral agency amounting to a willful breaking of a law (Moses 6:59). This would be a planned offense, a formality to serve an eternal purpose. The Prophet Lehi explained that "if Adam had not transgressed he would not have fallen" (2 Nephi 2:22) but would have remained in the same state in which he was created.

"And they would have had no children; wherefore they would have remained in a state of innocence, having no joy, for they knew no misery; doing no good, for they knew no sin" (2 Nephi 2:23).

But the Fall was planned, Lehi concludes, because "all things have been done in the wisdom of him who knoweth all things" (2 Nephi 2:24).

It was Eve who first transgressed the limits of Eden in order to initiate the conditions of mortality. Her act, whatever its nature, was formally a transgression but eternally a glorious necessity to open the doorway to eternal life. Adam showed his wisdom by doing the same. And thus Eve and "Adam fell that men might be" (2 Nephi 2:25).

Some Christians condemn Eve for her act, concluding that she and her daughters are somehow flawed by it. But Latter-day Saints, informed by revelation, celebrate Eve's act and honor her wisdom and courage in the great episode called the Fall.[3] Joseph Smith taught that Eve's act was not a "sin" because God had decreed it.[4] Brigham Young declared, "We should never blame Mother Eve, not the least."[5] And Elder Joseph Fielding Smith said, "I never speak of the part Eve took in this fall as a sin, nor do I accuse Adam of a sin. . . . This was a transgression of the law, but not a sin . . . for it was something that Adam and Eve had to do!"[6]

This suggested contrast between a *sin* and a *transgression* reminds us of the careful wording in the second article of faith: "We believe that men will be punished for their own *sins,* and not for Adam's *transgression*" (emphasis added). It also echoes a familiar distinction in the law. Some acts, like murder, are crimes because they are inherently wrong. Other acts, like operating without a license, are crimes only because they are legally prohibited. Under these distinctions, the act that produced the Fall was not a sin—inherently wrong—but a transgression—wrong because it was formally prohibited. These words are not always used to denote something different, but this distinction seems meaningful in the circumstances of the Fall.

Modern revelation shows that our first parents understood the necessity of the Fall. Adam declared, "Blessed be the name of God, for because of my transgression my eyes are opened, and in this life I shall have joy, and again in the flesh I shall see God" (Moses 5:10).

Note the different perspective and the special wisdom of Eve, who focused on the purpose and effect of the great plan of happiness: "Were it not for our transgression we never should have had seed, and never should have known good and evil, and the joy of our redemption, and the eternal life which God giveth unto all the obedient" (Moses 5:11). In his vision of the redemption of the dead, President Joseph F. Smith saw "the great and mighty ones" assembled to meet the Son of God, and among them was "our glorious Mother Eve" (D&C 138:38–39).

When we understand the plan of salvation, we also understand the purpose and effect of the commandments God has given His children. He teaches us correct principles and invites us to govern ourselves. We do this by the choices we make in mortality.

We live in a day when there are many political, legal, and social pressures for changes that confuse gender and homogenize the differences between men and women. Our eternal perspective sets us against changes that alter those separate duties and privileges of men and women that are essential to accomplish the great plan of happiness. We do not oppose all changes in the treatment of men and women, since some changes in laws or customs simply correct old wrongs that were never grounded in eternal principles.

The power to create mortal life is the most exalted power God has given His children. Its use was mandated in the first commandment, but another important commandment was given to forbid its misuse. The emphasis we place on the law of chastity is explained by our understanding of the purpose of our procreative powers in the accomplishment of God's plan.

The expression of our procreative powers is pleasing to God, but He has commanded that we confine it within the relationship of marriage. President Spencer W. Kimball taught, "In the context of lawful marriage, the intimacy of sexual relations is right and divinely approved. There is nothing unholy or degrading about sexuality in itself, for by that means men and women join in a process of creation and in an expression of love."[7]

Outside the bonds of marriage, all uses of procreative powers are to one degree or another a sinful degrading and perverting of the most divine attribute of men and women. The Book of Mormon teaches that unchastity is "most abominable above all sins save it be the shedding of innocent blood or denying the Holy Ghost" (Alma 39:5). In our own day, the First Presidency has declared as Church doctrine "that sexual sin—the illicit sexual relations of men and women—stands, in its enormity, next to murder."[8] Some who do not know the plan of salvation behave like promiscuous animals, but Latter-day Saints—especially those who are under sacred covenants—have no such latitude. We are solemnly responsible to God for the destruction or misuse of the creative powers he has placed within us.

The ultimate act of destruction is to take a life. That is why abortion is such a serious sin. Our attitude toward abortion is not based on revealed knowledge of when mortal life begins for legal purposes. It is fixed by our knowledge that according to an eternal plan all of the spirit children of God must come to this earth for a glorious purpose, and that individual identity began long before conception and will continue for all the eternities to come. We rely on the prophets of God, who have told us that while there may be "rare" exceptions, "the practice of elective abortion is fundamentally contrary to the Lord's injunction, 'Thou shalt not . . . kill, nor do anything like unto it' (D&C 59:6)."[9]

Our knowledge of the great plan of happiness also gives us a unique perspective on marriage and the bearing of children. In this we also run counter to some strong current forces in custom, law, and economics.

Marriage is disdained by an increasing number of couples, and many who marry choose to forgo children or place severe limits on their number. In recent years strong economic pressures in many nations have altered the traditional assumption of a single breadwinner per family. Increases in the number of working mothers of young children inevitably signal a reduced commitment of parental time to nurturing the young. The effect of these reductions is evident in the rising numbers of abortions, divorces, neglected children, and juvenile crimes.

The prophets teach that marriage is necessary to accomplish God's plan, to provide the approved setting for mortal birth, and to prepare family members for eternal life. The Lord said, "Marriage is ordained of God unto man . . . that the earth might answer the end of its creation; and that it might be filled with the measure of man, according to his creation before the world was made" (D&C 49:15–17).

Our concept of marriage is motivated by revealed truth, not by worldly sociology. The Apostle Paul taught, "Neither is the man without the woman, neither the woman without the man, in the Lord" (1 Corinthians 11:11). President Spencer W. Kimball explained, "Without proper and successful marriage, one will never be exalted."[10]

According to custom, men are expected to take the initiative in seeking marriage. That is why President Joseph F. Smith directed his prophetic pressure at men. He said, "No man who is marriageable is fully living his religion who remains unmarried."[11] We hear of some worthy LDS men in their thirties who are busy accumulating property and enjoying freedom from family responsibilities without any sense of urgency about marriage. Such brethren need to beware. They are deficient in a sacred duty.

Knowledge of the great plan of happiness also gives Latter-day Saints a distinctive attitude toward the bearing and nurturing of children. In some times and places, children have been regarded as no more than laborers in a family economic enterprise or as insurers of support for their parents. Though repelled by these repressions, some persons in our day have no compunctions against similar attitudes that subordinate the welfare of a spirit child of God to the comfort or convenience of parents.

The Savior taught that we should not lay up treasures on earth but rather that we should lay up treasures in heaven (Matthew 6:19–21). In light of the ultimate purpose of the great plan of happiness, I believe that the ultimate treasures on earth and in heaven are our children and our posterity.

President Kimball said, "It is an act of extreme selfishness for a married couple to refuse to have children when they are able to do so."[12] When married couples postpone childbearing until after they have satisfied their material goals, the mere passage of time assures that they seriously reduce their potential to participate in furthering our Heavenly Father's plan for all of his spirit children. Faithful Latter-day Saints cannot afford to look upon children as an interference with what the world calls "self-fulfillment." Our covenants with God and the ultimate purpose of life are tied up in those little ones who require our time, our love, and our sacrifice.

How many children should a couple have? All they can care for! Of course, to care for children means more than simply giving them life. Children must be loved, nurtured, taught, fed, clothed, housed, and well started in their capacities to be good parents themselves. Exercising faith in God's promises to bless them when they are keeping his commandments, many LDS parents have large families. Others seek but are not blessed with children or with the number of children they desire. In a matter as intimate as this, we should not judge one another.

President Gordon B. Hinckley gave this inspired counsel to an audience of young Latter-day Saints:

"I like to think of the positive side of the equation, of the meaning and sanctity of life, of the purpose of this estate in our eternal journey, of the need for the experiences of mortal life under the great plan of God our Father, of the joy that is to be found only where there are children in the home, of the blessings that come of good posterity. When I think of these values and see them taught and observed, then I am willing to leave the question of numbers to the man and the woman and the Lord."[13]

Some who are reading these words are probably saying, "But what about me?" We know that many worthy and wonderful Latter-day Saints currently lack the ideal opportunities and essential requirements for their progress. Singleness, childlessness, death, and divorce frustrate ideals and postpone the fulfillment of promised blessings. In addition, some women who desire to be full-time mothers and homemakers have been literally compelled to enter the full-time work force. But these frustrations are only temporary. The Lord has promised that in the eternities no blessing will be denied His sons and daughters who keep the commandments, are true to their covenants, and desire what is right.

Many of the most important deprivations of mortality will be set right in the Millennium, which is the time for fulfilling all that is incomplete in the great plan of happiness for all of our Father's worthy children. We know that will be true of temple ordinances. I believe it will also be true of family relationships and experiences.

I pray that we will not let the challenges and temporary diversions of mortality cause us to forget our covenants and lose sight of our eternal destiny. We who know God's plan for His children, we who have covenanted to participate, have a clear responsibility. We must desire to do what is right, and we must do all we can in our own circumstances in mortality.

In all of this, we should remember King Benjamin's caution to "see that all these things are done in wisdom and order; for it is not requisite that a man should run faster than he has strength" (Mosiah 4:27). I think of that inspired teaching whenever I feel inadequate, frustrated, or depressed.

When we have done all we are able, we can rely on God's promised mercy. We have a Savior who has taken upon Himself not just the sins but also "the pains and the sicknesses of his people . . . that he may know according to the flesh how to succor his people according to their infirmities" (Alma 7:11–12). He is our Savior, and when we have done all we can, He will make up the difference, in His own way and in His own time.

From an address published in the Ensign, *November 1993, 72–75.*

NOTES

1. Statement of the First Presidency, *Improvement Era,* March 1912, 417; see also Jeremiah 1:5.
2. *Millennial Star,* 24 August 1922, 539.
3. Bruce R. McConkie, *Woman,* Salt Lake City: Deseret Book, 1979, 67–68.
4. *The Words of Joseph Smith,* ed. Andrew F. Ehat and Lyndon W. Cook, Provo, Utah: Religious Studies Center, Brigham Young University, 1980, 63.
5. In *Journal of Discourses,* 26 vols., London: Latter-day Saints' Book Depot, 1854–86, 13:145.
6. *Doctrines of Salvation,* comp. Bruce R. McConkie, 3 vols., Salt Lake City: Bookcraft, 1954–56, 1:114–15.
7. *The Teachings of Spencer W. Kimball,* ed. Edward L. Kimball, Salt Lake City: Bookcraft, 1982, 311.
8. "Message of the First Presidency," 3 October 1942, as quoted in *Messages of the First Presidency of The Church of Jesus Christ of Latter-day Saints,* comp. James R. Clark, 6 vols., Salt Lake City: Bookcraft, 1965–75, 6:176.
9. *Supplement to the 1989 General Handbook of Instructions,* Salt Lake City: The Church of Jesus Christ of Latter-day Saints, 1991, 1.
10. *Marriage and Divorce,* Salt Lake City: Deseret Book, 1976, 24.
11. *Gospel Doctrine,* Salt Lake City: Deseret Book, 1939, 275.
12. "Fortify Your Homes Against Evil," *Ensign,* May 1979, 6.
13. "If I Were You, What Would I Do?" *Brigham Young University 1983–84 Fireside and Devotional Speeches,* Provo, Utah: University Publications, 1984, 11.

5

THE CHALLENGE
TO BECOME

THE APOSTLE PAUL TAUGHT THAT the Lord gave us teachings and teachers so that we might all attain "the measure of the stature of the fulness of Christ" (Ephesians 4:13). This process requires far more than acquiring knowledge. It is not even enough for us to be *convinced* by the gospel; we must act and think so that we are *converted* by it. In contrast to the institutions of the world, which teach us to *know* something, the gospel of Jesus Christ challenges us to *become* something.

Many Bible and modern scriptures speak of a final judgment at which all persons will be rewarded according to their deeds and the desires of their hearts. But other scriptures enlarge upon this by referring to our being judged by the *condition* we have achieved.

The prophet Nephi describes the final judgment in terms of what we *have become:* "And if their works have been filthiness they must needs *be* filthy; and if they *be* filthy it must needs be that they cannot dwell in the kingdom of God" (1 Nephi 15:33; emphasis added). Moroni declares, "He that *is* filthy shall be filthy still; and he that *is* righteous shall be righteous still" (Mormon 9:14; emphasis added; Revelation 22:11–12; 2 Nephi 9:16; D&C 88:35). The same would be true of "selfishness" or "disobedience" or any other personal attribute inconsistent with the requirements of God.

Referring to the state of the wicked in the final judgment, Alma explains that if we are condemned by our words, works, and thoughts, "we shall not be found spotless; . . . and in this awful state we shall not dare to look up to our God" (Alma 12:14).

From such teachings we conclude that the final judgment is not just an evaluation of a sum total of good and evil acts—what we have *done*. It is an acknowledgment of the final effect of our acts and thoughts—what we have *become*. It is not enough for anyone just to go through the motions. The commandments, ordinances, and covenants of the gospel are not a list of deposits required to be made in some heavenly account. The gospel of Jesus Christ is a plan that shows us how to become what our Heavenly Father desires us to become.

A parable illustrates this truth. A wealthy father knew that if he were to bestow his wealth upon a child who had not yet developed the needed wisdom and stature, the inheritance would probably be wasted. The father said to his child: "All that I have I desire to give you—not only my wealth but also my position and standing among men. That which I *have* I can easily give you, but that which I *am* you must obtain for yourself. You will qualify for your inheritance by learning what I have learned and by living as I have lived. I will give you the laws and principles by which I have acquired my wisdom and stature. Follow my example, mastering as I have mastered, and you will become as I am, and all that I have will be yours."

This parable parallels the pattern of heaven. The gospel of Jesus Christ promises the incomparable inheritance of eternal life—the fulness of the Father—and reveals the laws and principles by which it can be obtained.

We qualify for eternal life through a process of *conversion.* As used here, this word of many meanings signifies not just a convincing but also a profound change of nature. Jesus used this meaning when He taught His chief apostle the difference between a testimony and a conversion. Jesus asked His disciples, "Whom do men say that I the Son of man am?" Next He asked, "But whom say ye that I am?" (Matthew 16: 13, 15).

"And Simon Peter answered and said, Thou art the Christ, the Son of the living God. And Jesus answered and said unto him, Blessed art thou, Simon Bar-jona: for flesh and blood hath not revealed it unto thee, but my Father which is in heaven" (Matthew 16:16–17). Peter had a *testimony.* He knew that Jesus was the Christ, the promised Messiah, and he declared it. To *testify* is to know and to declare.

Later, Jesus taught these same men about *conversion,* which is far more than testimony. When the disciples asked who was the greatest in the kingdom of heaven, "Jesus called a little child unto him, and set him in the midst of them, and said, Verily I say unto you, Except ye be *converted,* and become as little children, ye shall not enter into the kingdom of heaven. Whosoever therefore shall humble himself as this little child, the same is greatest in the kingdom of heaven" (Matthew 18:2–4; emphasis added).

Still later, the Savior confirmed the importance of being converted, even for those with a testimony of the truth. In the sublime instructions given at the Last Supper, He told Simon Peter, "I have prayed for thee, that thy faith fail not: and when thou art converted, strengthen thy brethren" (Luke 22:32).

To strengthen his brethren—to nourish and lead the flock of God—this man who had followed Jesus for three years, who had been given the authority of the holy apostleship, who had been a valiant teacher and testifier of the Christian gospel, and whose testimony had caused the Master to declare him blessed still had to be *converted.*

The conversion Jesus requires of those who would enter the kingdom of heaven is far more than just being convinced to testify to the truthfulness of the gospel (Matthew 18:3). To testify is to *know* and to *declare.* But the gospel challenges us to be converted, which requires us to *do* and to *become.* If any of us relies solely upon our knowledge and testimony of the gospel, we are in the same position as the blessed but still unfinished apostles whom Jesus challenged to be converted. We all know someone who has a strong testimony but does not act upon it so as to be converted. For example, are our returned missionaries still seeking to be converted, or are some of them caught up in the ways of the world?

The needed conversion *by* the gospel begins with the introductory experience the scriptures call being "born again" (Mosiah 27:25; Alma 5:49; John 3:7; 1 Peter 1:23). By being baptized and receiving the gift of the Holy Ghost, we become the spiritual "sons and daughters" of Jesus Christ, "new creatures" who can "inherit the kingdom of God" (Mosiah 27:25–26).

In teaching the Nephites, the Savior referred to what they must become. He challenged them to repent and be baptized and to be sanctified by the reception of the Holy Ghost, that they "may stand spotless before me at the last day" (3 Nephi 27:20). He concluded, "Therefore, what manner of men ought ye to be? Verily I say unto you, even as I am" (3 Nephi 27:27).

The gospel of Jesus Christ is the plan by which we can become what children of God are supposed to become. This spotless and perfected state will result from a steady succession of covenants, ordinances, and actions—an accumulation of right choices and continuing repentance.

Because "this life is the time for men to prepare to meet God" (Alma 34:32), now is the time for each of us to work toward our personal conversion, toward becoming what our Heavenly Father desires us to become. As we do, we should remember that our family relationships—even more than our Church callings—are the setting in which the most important part of that development can occur. The conversion we must achieve requires us to be a good husband and father or a good wife and mother. Being a successful Church leader is not enough. Exaltation is an eternal family experience, and it is our mortal family experiences that are best suited to prepare us for it.

The Apostle John spoke of what we are challenged to become when he said, "Beloved, now are we the sons of God, and it doth not yet appear what we shall be: but we know that, when he shall appear, we shall be like him; for we shall see him as he is" (1 John 3:2; Moroni 7:48).

I hope the importance of conversion and becoming will cause our local leaders to reduce their concentration on statistical measures of actions and focus more on what our brothers and sisters *are* and what they are striving to *become*. Our needed conversions are often achieved more readily by suffering and adversity than by comfort and tranquility. Father Lehi promised his son Jacob that God would "consecrate [his] afflictions for [his] gain" (2 Nephi 2:2). The Prophet Joseph was promised that "thine adversity and thine afflictions shall be but a small moment; and then, if thou endure it well, God shall exalt thee on high" (D&C 121:7–8).

Most of us experience some measure of what the scriptures call "the furnace of affliction" (Isaiah 48:10; 1 Nephi 20:10). Some are submerged in service to a disadvantaged family member. Others suffer the death of a loved one or the loss or postponement of a righteous goal like marriage or childbearing. Still others struggle with personal impairments or with feelings of rejection, inadequacy, or depression. Through the justice and mercy of a loving Father in Heaven, the refinement and sanctification possible through such experiences can help make us what God desires us to become.

We are challenged to move through a process of conversion

toward that status and condition called eternal life. This is achieved not just by doing what is right but also by doing it for the right reason—for the pure love of Christ. The Apostle Paul illustrated this in his famous teaching about the importance of charity (1 Corinthians 13). The reason charity never fails and the reason charity is greater than even the most significant acts of goodness he cited is that charity, "the pure love of Christ" (Moroni 7:47), is not an *act* but a *condition,* or state of being. Charity is attained through a succession of acts that result in conversion. Charity is something one becomes. Thus, as Moroni declared, "except men shall *have* charity they cannot inherit" the place prepared for them in the mansions of the Father (Ether 12:34; emphasis added).

All of this helps us understand an important meaning of the parable of the laborers in the vineyard, which the Savior gave to explain what the kingdom of heaven is like. The owner of the vineyard hired laborers at different times of the day. Some he sent into the vineyard early in the morning, others about the third hour, and others in the sixth and ninth hours. Finally, in the eleventh hour he sent others into the vineyard, promising that he would also pay them "whatsoever is right" (Matthew 20:7).

At the end of the day the owner of the vineyard gave the same wage to every worker, even to those who had come in the eleventh hour. When those who had worked the entire day saw this, "they murmured against the goodman of the house" (Matthew 20:11). The owner did not yield but merely pointed out that he had done no one any wrong, since he had paid each man the agreed amount.

Like other parables, this one can teach several different and valuable principles. For present purposes its lesson is that the Master's reward in the final judgment will not be based on how long we have labored in the vineyard. We do not obtain our heavenly reward by punching a time clock. What is essential is that our labors in the workplace of the Lord have caused us to *become* something. This requires more time for some than for others.

What is important in the end is what we have become by our labors. Many who come in the eleventh hour have been refined and prepared by the Lord in ways other than formal employment in the vineyard. These workers are like the prepared dry mix to which it is only necessary to add water—the perfecting ordinance of baptism and the gift of the Holy Ghost. With that addition, even in the eleventh hour, these workers are in the same state of development and are qualified to receive the same reward as those who have labored long in the vineyard.

This parable teaches us that we should never give up hope and loving associations with family members and friends whose fine qualities evidence their progress toward what a loving Father would have them become (Moroni 7:5–14). Similarly, the power of the Atonement and the principle of repentance show that we should never give up on loved ones who are now making many wrong choices.

Instead of being judgmental about others, we should be concerned about ourselves. We must not give up on ourselves or stop striving to improve. We are children of God, and it is possible for us to become what our Heavenly Father would have us become.

How can we measure our progress? The scriptures suggest various ways. I mention only two.

After King Benjamin's great sermon, many of his hearers cried out that the spirit of the Lord "has wrought a mighty change in us, or in our hearts, that we have no more disposition to do evil, but to do good continually" (Mosiah 5:2). If we are losing our desire to do evil, we are progressing toward our heavenly goal.

The Apostle Paul said that persons who have received the spirit of God "have the mind of Christ" (1 Corinthians 2:16). I understand this to mean that persons who are proceeding toward the needed conversion are beginning to see things as our Heavenly Father and His Son, Jesus Christ, see them. They are hearing His voice instead of the voice of the world, and they are doing things in His way instead of by the ways of the world.

I testify of Jesus Christ, our Savior and our Redeemer, whose Church this is. I testify with gratitude of the plan of the Father under which, through the resurrection and atonement of our Savior, we have the assurance of immortality and the opportunity to become what is necessary for eternal life.

———

From an address published in the Ensign, *November 2000, 32–34.*

6

POWERFUL IDEAS

DURING THE FUNERAL OF AN ELECT lady, a speaker described three of her great qualities: loyalty, obedience, and faith. As he elaborated on her life, I thought how appropriate it was to speak of such powerful qualities in a funeral tribute. A life is not a trivial thing, and its passing should not be memorialized with trivial things. A funeral service is a time to speak of powerful ideas—ideas that can appropriately stand beside the importance of life, ideas that are powerful in their influence on those who remain behind.

As I enjoyed the spirit of this inspiring funeral, I directed my thoughts toward the application of this principle in other settings. Parents should also teach powerful ideas. So should home teachers, visiting teachers, and the teachers in various classes. The Savior warned that we will be judged for "every idle word that [we] shall speak" (Matthew 12:36). Modern revelation commands us to cease from "light speeches" and "light-mindedness" (D&C

88:121) and to cast away "idle thoughts" and "excess of laughter" (D&C 88:69). There are plenty of spokesmen for trivial things. Latter-day Saints, on the other hand, should be constantly concerned with teaching and emphasizing those great and powerful eternal truths that will help us find our way back to the presence of our Heavenly Father.

More than thirty years ago, I saw a scholarly book on "general education"—the body of knowledge expected of all educated persons. Its title, *The Knowledge Most Worth Having*,[1] continues to remind us that all knowledge is not of equal value. Some knowledge is more important than other knowledge. That principle also applies to what we call spiritual knowledge.

Consider the power of the idea taught in our beloved song "I Am a Child of God."[2] Here is the answer to one of life's great questions, "Who am I?" I am a child of God with a spirit lineage to heavenly parents. Knowledge of that parentage defines our eternal potential. That powerful idea is a potent antidepressant. It can strengthen each of us to make righteous choices and to seek the best that is within us. Establish in the mind of a young person the idea that he or she is a child of God and you have given self-respect and motivation to move against the problems of life.

When we understand our relationship to God, we also understand our relationship to one another. All men and women on the earth are the offspring of God—spirit brothers and sisters. What a powerful idea! No wonder God's Only Begotten Son commanded us to love one another. If only we could do so! What a different world it would be if brotherly and sisterly love and unselfish assistance could transcend all boundaries of nation, creed, and color. Such love would not erase all differences of opinion and action, but it would encourage each of us to focus our opposition on actions rather than on actors.

The eternal truth that our Heavenly Father loves all His children is an immensely powerful idea. It is especially powerful when children can visualize it through the love and sacrifice of their earthly parents. Love is the most powerful force in the world. Arthur Henry King said, "Love is not just an ecstasy, not just an intense feeling. It is a driving force. It is something that carries us through our life of joyful duty."[3] We all have our own examples of the power of love. Many years ago I recorded some memories I had of my father, who died before I was eight years old. What I wrote then illustrates the power of love in the life of a boy:

"The strongest impression I have of my relationship with my father I cannot document with any event or any words I can recall. It is a feeling. Based on words and actions long since lost to mind, this feeling persists with all the clarity of perfect faith. He loved me and he was proud of me. . . . That is the kind of memory a boy can treasure, and also a man."[4]

Another powerful idea we should teach one another is that mortal life has a purpose and that mortal death is not the end but only a transition to the next phase of an existence that is immortal. President Brigham Young taught that "our existence here is for the sole purpose of exaltation and restoration to the presence of our Father and God."[5] The idea of eternal progress is one of the most powerful ideas in our theology. It gives us hope when we falter and it challenges us when we soar. Surely this is one of the great "solemnities of eternity" that we are commanded to let "rest upon [our] minds" (D&C 43:34).

Another powerful idea that lifts us from discouragement is that the work of The Church of Jesus Christ of Latter-day Saints, "to bring to pass the . . . eternal life of man" (Moses 1:39), is an eternal work. Not all problems are overcome and not all needed relationships are fixed in mortality. The work of salvation goes on beyond the veil of death, and we should not be too apprehensive about incompleteness within the limits of mortality.

A powerful idea with immediate practical application is the reality that we can pray to our Heavenly Father, and He will hear our prayers and help us in the way that is best for us. Most of us have experienced the terrible empty feeling that comes from being separated from those who love us. If we remember that we can pray and be heard and helped, we can always withstand that feeling of emptiness. We can always be in touch with a powerful friend who loves us and helps us, in His own time and in His own way.

Thousands of experiences show that we can pray and have our prayers answered. Some of the choicest involve young children. In the biography of President Spencer W. Kimball we read:

"Again and again Spencer watched his parents take their problems to the Lord. One day when Spencer was five and out doing his chores, little one-year-old Fannie wandered from the house and was lost. No one could find her. Clare, sixteen, said, 'Ma, if we pray, the Lord will direct us to Fannie.' So the mother and children prayed. Immediately after the prayer Gordon walked to the very spot where Fannie was fast asleep in a large box behind the chicken coop. 'We thanked our Heavenly Father over and over,' Olive recorded in her journal."[6]

Every follower of Jesus Christ knows that the most powerful ideas of the Christian faith are the resurrection and the atonement of Jesus Christ. Because of Him we can be forgiven of our sins, and we will live again. Those powerful ideas have been explained in countless sermons from Latter-day Saint pulpits. They are well known but not well applied in the lives of most of us.

Our model is not the latest popular hero of sport or entertainment, nor those who accumulate property, prestige, or expensive toys—diversions that encourage us to concentrate on what is temporary and forget what is eternal. Our model, our first priority, is Jesus Christ. We must testify of Him and teach one another how we can apply His teachings and His example in our lives.

President Young gave us some practical advice on how to do this. "The difference between God and the Devil," he said, "is that God creates and organizes, while the whole study of the

Devil is to destroy."[7] In that contrast we have an important example of the reality of "opposition in all things" (2 Nephi 2:11).

Remember, our Savior, Jesus Christ, always builds us up and never tears us down. We should apply the power of that example in the ways we use our time, including our recreation and diversions. Consider the themes of the books, magazines, movies, television shows, and music we make popular by our patronage. Do the purposes and actions portrayed in our chosen entertainment build up or tear down the children of God? During my lifetime I have seen a strong trend to displace what builds up and dignifies the children of God with portrayals and performances that are depressing, demeaning, and destructive.

The powerful idea in this example is that whatever builds people up serves the cause of the Master, and whatever tears people down serves the cause of the adversary. We support one cause or the other every day by our patronage. This should remind us of our responsibility and motivate us toward fulfilling it in a way that would be pleasing to Him whose suffering offers us hope and whose example gives us direction.

We should always put the Savior first. The first commandment Jehovah gave to the children of Israel was, "Thou shalt have no other gods before me" (Exodus 20:3). This seems like a simple idea, but in practice many find it difficult.

It is surprisingly easy to take what should be our first devotion and subordinate it to other priorities. More than fifty years ago, the Christian philosopher C. S. Lewis illustrated that tendency with an example that is distressingly applicable in our own day. In his book *The Screwtape Letters,* a senior devil explains how to corrupt Christians and frustrate the work of Jesus Christ. One letter explains how any "extreme devotion" can lead Christians away from the Lord and the practice of Christianity. Lewis gives two examples, extreme patriotism and extreme pacifism, and explains how either extreme devotion can corrupt its adherent.

"Let him begin by treating the Patriotism or the Pacifism as a part of his religion. Then let him, under the influence of partisan spirit, come to regard it as the most important part. Then quietly and gradually nurse him on to the stage at which the religion becomes merely part of the 'cause,' in which Christianity is valued chiefly because of the excellent arguments it can produce in favour of the British war effort or of pacifism. . . . Once you have made the World an end, and faith a means, you have almost won your man, and it makes very little difference what kind of worldly end he is pursuing."[8]

We can readily see that tendency in our own time, with many causes that, while good in themselves, become spiritually corrupting when they assume priorities ahead of Him who commanded, "Thou shalt have no other gods before me." Jesus Christ and His work come first. Anything that would use Him or His kingdom or His church as a means to an end serves the cause of the adversary.

Two other powerful ideas were given voice by a noble young woman who survived a terrible experience. Virginia Reed was a survivor of the tragic Donner-Reed party, which made one of the earliest wagon treks into California. If members of this wagon train had followed the established Oregon Trail from Fort Bridger, Wyoming, northwest to Fort Hall, Idaho, and then southwest toward California, they would have reached their destination in safety. Instead, they were misled by a promoter. Lansford W. Hastings persuaded them that they could save significant distance and time by following his so-called Hastings Cutoff. The Donner-Reed party left the proven trail at Fort Bridger and struggled southwest. They blazed a trail through the rugged Wasatch Mountains, traveled south of the Great Salt Lake, and then headed westward in furnace heat over the soggy surface of the salt flats.

The numerous delays and incredible energies expended on this unproven route cost the Donner-Reed party an extra month in reaching the Sierra Nevada Mountains. As they hastened up the eastern slope trying to beat the first snows, they were caught in a tragic winter storm only one day short of the summit and a downhill passage into California. Marooned for the winter, the party lost half their group from starvation and cold.

After months in the mountains and incredible hardships of hunger and terror, thirteen-year-old Virginia Reed reached California and sent a letter to her cousin in the Midwest. After recounting her experiences and the terrible sufferings of the party, she concluded with this wise advice: "Never take no cutofs and hury along as fast as you can."[9]

That is powerful and true advice, especially for teenagers. Young people are surrounded by many beckoning paths and many persuasive promoters who offer advice and cutoffs as substitutes for the proven way. "Try out this detour" or "Tarry here for a while" are familiar proposals on the journey of life. But we must remember Virginia Reed's advice: "Never take no cutofs and hury along as fast as you can."

I conclude with an example from the life of the Apostle Paul. During his ministry he was exposed to ample light-mindedness, idle thoughts, and trivial things. In Athens he observed that "all the Athenians and strangers which were there [in the market] spent their time in nothing else, but . . . to tell, or to hear some new thing" (Acts 17:21). Paul's determination to focus on powerful ideas is evident in one of his letters to the Saints in Corinth. He had not come "with excellency of speech or of wisdom," he reminded them. "For I determined not to know any thing among you, save Jesus Christ, and him crucified" (1 Corinthians 2:1–2).

Let us follow the commandments of God and the example of His servants. Let us focus our teachings on those great and powerful ideas that have eternal significance in promoting righteousness, building up the children of God, and helping each of us toward our destiny of eternal life.

From an address published in the Ensign, *November 1995, 25–27.*

NOTES

1. Wayne C. Booth, ed., Chicago: The University of Chicago Press, 1967.
2. *Hymns of the Church of Jesus Christ of Latter-day Saints,* Salt Lake City: The Church of Jesus Christ of Latter-day Saints, 1985, no. 301.
3. *The Abundance of the Heart,* Salt Lake City: Bookcraft, 1986, 84.
4. "Memories of My Father," 15 October 1967; manuscript in possession of author.
5. *Discourses of Brigham Young,* sel. John A. Widtsoe, Salt Lake City: Deseret Book, 1978, 37.
6. Edward L. Kimball and Andrew E. Kimball Jr., *Spencer W. Kimball,* Salt Lake City: Bookcraft, 1977, 31.
7. *Discourses of Brigham Young,* sel. John A. Widtsoe, Salt Lake City: Deseret Book, 1976, 69.
8. *The Screwtape Letters,* rev. ed., New York: Macmillan, 1982, 35.
9. Letter from Virginia E. B. Reed to her cousin Mary Gillespie, 16 May 1847; quoted in *West from Fort Bridger,* ed. J. Roderic Korns and Dale L. Morgan, Logan, Utah: Utah State University Press, 1994, 238.

7

THE RESURRECTION

THE BOOK OF JOB POSES THE universal question, "If a man die, shall he live again?" (Job 14:14). The question of resurrection from the dead is a central subject of scripture, ancient and modern. The resurrection is a pillar of our faith. It adds meaning to our doctrine, motivation to our behavior, and hope for our future.

The universal resurrection became a reality with the resurrection of Jesus Christ (Matthew 27:52–53). On the third day after His death and burial, Jesus came forth out of the tomb. He appeared to several men and women, and then to the assembled apostles. Three of the Gospels describe this event. Luke is the most complete:

"Jesus . . . saith unto them, Peace be unto you. But they were terrified and affrighted, and supposed that they had seen a spirit.

"And he said unto them, Why are ye troubled? And why do thoughts arise in your hearts? Behold my hands and my feet, that it is I myself: handle me, and see; for a spirit hath not flesh and bones, as ye see me have. . . .

"Then opened he their understanding, . . . and said unto them, Thus it is written, and thus it behoved Christ to suffer, and to rise from the dead the third day" (Luke 24:36–39, 45–46).

The Savior gave the apostles a second witness. Thomas, one of the Twelve, had not been with them when Jesus came. He insisted that he would not believe unless he could see and feel for himself. John records:

"And after eight days again his disciples were within, and Thomas with them: then came Jesus, the doors being shut, and stood in the midst, and said, Peace be unto you.

"Then saith he to Thomas, Reach hither thy finger, and behold my hands; and reach hither thy hand, and thrust it into my side: and be not faithless, but believing. And Thomas answered and said unto him, My Lord and my God.

"Jesus saith unto him, Thomas, because thou hast seen me, thou hast believed: blessed are they that have not seen, and yet have believed" (John 20:26–29).

Despite these biblical witnesses, many who call themselves Christians reject or confess serious doubts about the reality of the Savior's resurrection. As if to anticipate and counter such doubts, the Bible records many appearances of the risen Christ. In some of these, He appeared to a single individual, such as to Mary Magdalene at the sepulchre. In others He appeared to large or small groups, such as when "he was seen of [about] five hundred brethren at once" (1 Corinthians 15:6).

The Book of Mormon: Another Testament of Jesus Christ records the experience of hundreds who saw the risen Lord in person and touched Him, feeling the prints of the nails in His hands and feet and thrusting their hands into His side. The Savior invited a multitude to have this experience "one by one" so that they could know that He was "the God of Israel, and the God of the whole earth, and [had] been slain for the sins of the world" (3 Nephi 11:15, 14).

During the course of His personal ministry among these faithful people, the resurrected Christ healed the sick and also "took their little children, one by one, and blessed them" (3 Nephi 17:21). This tender episode was witnessed by about 2,500 men, women, and children (3 Nephi 17:25).

The possibility that a *mortal* who has died will be brought forth and live again in a resurrected body has awakened hope and stirred controversy through much of recorded history. Relying on clear scriptural teachings, Latter-day Saints join in affirming that Christ has "broken the bands of death" (Mosiah 16:7) and that "death is swallowed up in victory" (1 Corinthians 15:54; Mormon 7:5; Mosiah 15:8; 16:7–8; Alma 22:14). Because we believe the Bible and Book of Mormon descriptions of the literal resurrection of Jesus Christ, we also readily accept the numerous scriptural teachings that a similar resurrection will come to all mortals who have ever lived upon this earth (1 Corinthians 15:22; 2 Nephi 9:22; Helaman 14:17; Mormon 9:13; D&C 29:26; 76:39, 42–44). As Jesus taught, "Because I live, ye shall live also" (John 14:19).

The literal and universal nature of the resurrection is vividly described in the Book of Mormon. The prophet Amulek taught:

"The death of Christ shall loose the bands of this temporal death, that all shall be raised from this temporal death. The spirit and the body shall be reunited again in its perfect form; both limb and joint shall be restored to its proper frame, even as we now are at this time; . . .

"Now, this restoration shall come to all, both old and young, both bond and free, both male and female, both the wicked and the righteous; and even there shall not so much as a hair of their heads be lost; but every thing shall be restored to its perfect frame" (Alma 11:42–44).

Alma also taught that in the resurrection "all things shall be restored to their proper and perfect frame" (Alma 40:23).

Many living witnesses can testify to the literal fulfillment of these scriptural assurances of the resurrection. Many, including some in my own extended family, have seen a departed family member in vision or personal appearance and have witnessed that loved one's restoration in "proper and perfect frame" in the prime of life. Whether these were manifestations of persons already resurrected or of righteous spirits awaiting an assured resurrection, the reality and nature of the resurrection of mortals is evident.

What a comfort to know that all who have been disadvantaged in life from birth defects, from mortal injuries, from disease, or from the natural deterioration of old age will be resurrected in "proper and perfect frame."

I wonder if we fully appreciate the enormous significance of our belief in a literal, universal resurrection. The assurance of immortality is fundamental to our faith. The Prophet Joseph Smith declared:

"The fundamental principles of our religion are the testimony of the Apostles and Prophets, concerning Jesus Christ, that He died, was buried, and rose again the third day, and ascended into heaven; and all other things which pertain to our religion are only appendages to it."[1]

Of all things in the Savior's ministry, why did the Prophet Joseph Smith use the testimony of the Savior's death, burial, and resurrection as the fundamental principle of our religion, saying that "all other things . . . are only appendages to it"? The answer is found in the fact that the Savior's resurrection is central to what the prophets have called "the great and eternal plan of deliverance from death" (2 Nephi 11:5).

In our eternal journey, the resurrection is the mighty milepost that signifies the end of mortality and the beginning of immortality. The Lord described the importance of this vital transition when He declared, "And thus did I, the Lord God, appoint unto man the days of his probation—that by his natural death he might be raised in immortality unto eternal life, even as many as would believe" (D&C 29:43). Similarly, the Book of Mormon teaches, "For as death hath passed upon all men, to fulfil the merciful plan of the great Creator, there must needs be a power of resurrection" (2 Nephi 9:6). We also know, from modern revelation, that without the reuniting of our spirits and our bodies in the resurrection we could not receive a "fulness of joy" (D&C 93:33–34).

When we understand the vital position of the resurrection in the "plan of redemption" that governs our eternal journey (Alma 12:25), we see why the Apostle Paul taught, "If there be no resurrection of the dead, then . . . is our preaching vain, and your faith is also vain" (1 Corinthians 15:13–14). We also see why the Apostle Peter referred to the fact that God the Father, in His abundant mercy, "hath begotten us again unto a lively hope by the resurrection of Jesus Christ from the dead" (1 Peter 1:3; 1 Thessalonians 4:13–18).

The "lively hope" we are given by the resurrection is our conviction that death is not the conclusion of our identity but merely a necessary step in our destined transition from mortality to immortality. This hope changes the whole perspective of mortal life. The assurance of resurrection and immortality affects how we look on the physical challenges of mortality, how we live our mortal lives, and how we relate to those around us.

The assurance of resurrection gives us the strength and perspective to endure the mortal challenges we and those we love face—such things as the physical, mental, or emotional deficiencies we bring with us at birth or acquire during mortal life. Because of the resurrection, we know that these mortal deficiencies are only temporary!

The assurance of resurrection also gives us a powerful incentive to keep the commandments of God during our mortal lives. Resurrection is much more than merely reuniting a spirit to a body held captive by the grave. We know from the Book of Mormon that the resurrection is a *restoration* that brings back "carnal for carnal" and "good for that which is good" (Alma 41:13; 41:2–4; Helaman 14:31). The prophet Amulek taught, "That same spirit which doth possess your bodies at the time that ye go out of this life, that same spirit will have power to possess your body in that eternal world" (Alma 34:34). As a result, when we leave this life and go on to the next life, "they who are righteous shall be righteous still" (2 Nephi 9:16), and "whatever principle of intelligence we attain unto in this life . . . will rise with us in the resurrection" (D&C 130:18).

The principle of restoration also means that those who are not righteous in mortal life will not rise up righteous in the resurrection (2 Nephi 9:16; 1 Corinthians 15:35–44; D&C 88:27–32). Moreover, unless our mortal sins have been cleansed and blotted out by repentance and forgiveness (Alma 5:21; 2 Nephi 9:45–46; D&C 58:42), we will be resurrected with a "bright recollection" (Alma 11:43) and a "perfect knowledge of all of our guilt, and our uncleanness" (2 Nephi 9:14; Alma 5:18). The seriousness of that reality is emphasized by the many scriptures suggesting that the resurrection is followed immediately by the Final Judgment (2 Nephi 9:15, 22; Mosiah 26:25; Alma 11:43–44; 42:23; Mormon 7:6; 9:13–14). Truly, "this life is the time for men to prepare to meet God" (Alma 34:32).

The assurance that the resurrection will include an opportunity to be with our family members—husband, wife, parents, brothers and sisters, children, and grandchildren—is a powerful encouragement for us to fulfill our family responsibilities in mortality. It helps us live together in love in this life in anticipation of joyful reunions and associations in the next.

Our sure knowledge of a resurrection to immortality also gives us the courage to face our own death—even a death that we might call premature. Thus, the people of Ammon in the Book of Mormon "never did look upon death with any degree of terror, for their hope and views of Christ and the resurrection; therefore, death was swallowed up to them by the victory of Christ over it" (Alma 27:28).

The assurance of immortality also helps us bear the mortal separations involved in the death of our loved ones. Every one of us has wept at a death, grieved through a funeral, or stood in pain at a graveside. I am surely one who has. We should all praise God for the assured resurrection that makes our mortal separations temporary and gives us the hope and strength to carry on.

We are living in a glorious season of temple building. This is also a consequence of our faith in the resurrection. While accompanying President Hinckley at the dedication of a new temple, I heard him say in that sacred setting: "Temples stand as a witness of our conviction of immortality. Our temples are concerned with life beyond the grave. For example, there is no need for marriage in the temple if we were only concerned with being married for the period of our mortal lives."

This prophetic teaching enlarged my understanding. Our temples are living, working testimonies to our faith in the reality of the resurrection. They provide the sacred settings where living proxies can perform all of the necessary ordinances of mortal life in behalf of those who live in the world of spirits. None of this would be meaningful if we did not have the assurance of universal immortality and the opportunity for eternal life because of the resurrection of our Lord and Savior, Jesus Christ.

We believe in the literal, universal resurrection of all mankind because of "the resurrection of the Holy One of Israel" (2 Nephi 9:12). We also testify of "The Living Christ," as the apostolic declaration of the same name proclaims:

"We solemnly testify that His life, which is central to all human history, neither began in Bethlehem nor concluded on Calvary. . . .

"We bear testimony, as His duly ordained Apostles—that Jesus is the Living Christ, the immortal Son of God. He is the great King Immanuel, who stands today on the right hand of His Father. He is the light, the life, and the hope of the world. His way is the path that leads to happiness in this life and eternal life in the world to come."[2]

From an address published in the Ensign, *May 2000, 14–16.*

NOTES

1. *Teachings of the Prophet Joseph Smith,* sel. Joseph Fielding Smith, Salt Lake City: Deseret Book, 1976, 121.

2. "The Living Christ: The Testimony of the Apostles," *Ensign,* April 2000, 2–3.

8

ANOTHER TESTAMENT
OF JESUS CHRIST

PRESIDENT EZRA TAFT BENSON'S administration as president
of the Church was punctuated by his repeated and fervent
pleas for all of us to study the Book of Mormon on a daily basis
for the rest of our lives. For example, in his conference address to
the members of the Church during the Solemn Assembly where
he was sustained as president of the Church, he said:

"The Lord inspired His servant Lorenzo Snow to reemphasize the principle of tithing to redeem the Church from financial
bondage. . . . Now, in our day, the Lord has revealed the need to
reemphasize the Book of Mormon to get the Church and all the
children of Zion out from under condemnation—the scourge and
judgment. This message must be carried to the members of the
Church throughout the world."[1]

As in that important first address, President Benson often
referred to the condemnation the eighty-fourth section of the

Doctrine and Covenants describes as being imposed on the Saints for their neglect of the Book of Mormon. This revelation was given to the Church in September 1832, just two and one-half years after the Church was organized. In verses 43–44, the Lord declared:

"And I now give unto you a commandment to beware concerning yourselves, to give diligent heed to the words of eternal life. For you shall live by every word that proceedeth forth from the mouth of God."

Verses 45–47 affirm the truth of the word of the Lord and of the enlightenment given to all by the Spirit, and the fact that all who hearken to the Spirit come unto God the Father. Verse 48 then refers to the gospel covenant:

"And the Father teacheth him of the covenant which he has renewed and confirmed upon you, which is confirmed upon you for your sakes, and not for your sakes only, but for the sake of the whole world."

Verses 49 through 53 describe the sin and darkness of those who do not come to God and hearken to His voice.

The succeeding verses, 54–58, describe the circumstance of some early members of the Church:

"And your minds in times past have been darkened because of unbelief, and because you have treated lightly the things you have received—which vanity and unbelief have brought the whole church under condemnation. And this condemnation resteth upon the children of Zion, even all.

"And they shall remain under this condemnation until they repent and remember the new covenant, even the Book of Mormon and the former commandments which I have given them, not only to say, but to do according to that which I have written—that they may bring forth fruit meet for their Father's kingdom; otherwise there remaineth a scourge and judgment to be poured out upon the children of Zion."

Along with other General Authorities, I have a clear recollection of the General Authority temple meeting held March 5,

1987. For a year, President Benson had been stressing the reading of the Book of Mormon. Repeatedly he had quoted these verses from the Doctrine and Covenants, including the Lord's statement that the Saints' conduct had "brought the whole church under condemnation" (D&C 84:55).

In that temple meeting, President Benson reread those statements and declared, "His condemnation has not been lifted, nor will it be until we repent." President Benson also repeated his declaration of a year earlier that "in our day the Lord has inspired His servant to reemphasize the Book of Mormon to get the Church out from under condemnation."

Along with others, I felt the impact of this declaration of condemnation. As I studied the subject, I was relieved to find that the serious consequences of this condemnation need not be permanent. The use of this term elsewhere in modern revelation suggests that it refers to a punishment or a penalty, not to a permanent banishment (D&C 82:3). In fact, the words President Benson quoted invite the Saints to repent of their deficiencies so the condemnation can be removed.

To understand why President Benson exhorted us to reemphasize the Book of Mormon and why this is necessary to remove us from condemnation, we need to remember the major theme of that book. In his many messages about the Book of Mormon, President Benson taught us that the major significance of the Book of Mormon is its witness of Jesus Christ as the Only Begotten Son of God the Eternal Father, who redeemed and saved us from death and sin. It explains our Savior's atonement, which is the most fundamental doctrine of our faith.

In his conference address in October 1981, President Benson emphasized that the "major purpose" of the record that became the Book of Mormon "is to convince a later generation that Jesus is the Christ, the Son of God."[2] Two years after he became president of the Church, he repeated that characterization in a marvelous talk titled "Come unto Christ." In that talk, he declared that "the major mission of the Book of Mormon . . . is 'to the convincing of the Jew and Gentile that Jesus is the Christ.' "[3]

In the General Authority meeting mentioned above, President Benson distributed some materials to assist us in carrying his Book of Mormon message throughout the world. Included in that distribution were copies of the talk he gave during the April 1975 general conference, "The Book of Mormon Is the Word of God." I underlined these words from that important talk:

"Now, we have not been using the Book of Mormon as we should. Our homes are not as strong unless we are using it to bring our children to Christ. . . . Social, ethical, cultural, or educational converts will not survive under the heat of the day unless their taproots go down to the fulness of the gospel which the Book of Mormon contains."[4]

President Benson frequently reminded us of the Prophet Joseph Smith's declaration that the Book of Mormon is "the keystone of our religion, and a man would get nearer to God by abiding by its precepts, than by any other book."[5] In a landmark address during the first year of his service as president of the Church, President Benson explained two ways in which the Book of Mormon is the keystone of our religion.

"The Book of Mormon is the keystone in our witness of Jesus Christ, who is himself the cornerstone of everything we do. . . . Its testimony of the Master is clear, undiluted, and full of power. . . . The Book of Mormon is also the keystone of the doctrine of the Resurrection."[6]

Note that both of these ways in which the Book of Mormon is the keystone of our religion focus on our relationship to Christ—our witness of Him and our testimony of His atonement and resurrection.

In addition, President Benson often reminded us of the Lord's declarations through the Prophet Joseph Smith that the Book of Mormon is "the most correct of any book on earth"[7] and that it "contains . . . the fulness of the gospel of Jesus Christ" (D&C 20:9). This does not mean that the Book of Mormon contains a full explanation of every principle of the gospel. What it means, President Benson explained, is that "in the Book of Mormon we will find the fullness of those doctrines required for our salvation." Most significantly, he noted, "It also provides the most complete explanation of the doctrine of the Atonement."[8]

Having reminded ourselves of the major theme and purpose of the Book of Mormon, we can proceed to consider why we have been directed to intensify our study of it at this time. I have carefully considered all of the reasons President Benson gave for studying the Book of Mormon, including many reasons that it is uniquely important in our day. From this perspective and from the frequent opportunities I had to listen to him in our council meetings, I offer my clear impressions of why he pleaded with us to repent of our neglect of the Book of Mormon.

One reason stands out above all the rest. Expressly and by implication, President Benson affirmed that this subject is the most important of all. I believe that it was the neglect—the "treating lightly"—of this subject that brought the early Church under condemnation. I believe it is the neglect of this subject that has continued the condemnation in our own day. Though supremely important, this subject is so simple that it is easy for us to neglect it in favor of other things. The subject I believe we have neglected is the Book of Mormon's witness of the divinity and mission of Jesus Christ and our covenant relationship to Him.

In the opening session of October 1986 general conference, President Benson read the verses from the Doctrine and Covenants about the whole church being under condemnation and remaining so "until they repent and remember the new covenant, even the Book of Mormon" (D&C 84:57). In speaking of this, he likened the word *covenant* to *testament,* as in the "New Testament." He reminded us that the Book of Mormon "is indeed another testament or witness of Jesus," adding that this was "one of the reasons why we have recently added the words 'Another Testament of Jesus Christ' to the title of the Book of Mormon."[9]

Later in that same message, President Benson repeated words he had given in an earlier talk. Note the point of emphasis:

"Do eternal consequences rest upon our response to this book? Yes, either to our blessing or our condemnation. Every Latter-day Saint should make the study of this book a lifetime pursuit. Otherwise he is placing his soul in jeopardy and neglecting that which could give spiritual and intellectual unity to his whole life. There is a difference between a convert who is built on the rock of Christ through the Book of Mormon and stays hold of that iron rod, and one who is not."[10]

That is the key: to use the Book of Mormon to become "built on the rock of Christ"! The Book of Mormon is a testament of Jesus Christ. It explains the significance of His atonement and the content of our covenant relationship with Him.

President Benson stressed this key point again and again in his messages as president of the Church:

"What is the major purpose of the Book of Mormon? To bring men to Christ and to be reconciled to Him."[11]

"The Book of Mormon brings men to Christ. [It] tells in a plain manner of Christ and His gospel. It testifies of His divinity and of the necessity for a Redeemer and the need of our putting trust in Him. . . .

"The Book of Mormon is the great standard we are to use. . . . It contains the words of Christ, and its great mission is to bring men to Christ, and all other things are secondary. The golden question of the Book of Mormon is, 'Do you want to learn more of Christ?'"[12]

"No one adequately and properly knows why he needs Christ until he understands and accepts the doctrine of the Fall and its effect upon all mankind. And no other book in the world explains this vital doctrine nearly as well as the Book of Mormon. . . .

"Do we understand and are we effective in teaching and preaching the Atonement? What personal meaning does the Lord's suffering in Gethsemane and on Calvary have for each of us? . . .

"Now, what should be the source for teaching the great plan of the Eternal God? The scriptures, of course—particularly the Book of Mormon. . . .

"Let us read the Book of Mormon and be convinced that Jesus is the Christ. Let us continually reread the Book of Mormon so that we might more fully come to Christ, be committed to Him, centered in Him, and consumed in Him."[13]

We can clearly see the harmony in all this. The Book of Mormon is Christ-centered. That is its essential feature and that is the reason we are commanded to study it continually. We must use the Book of Mormon to bring us to Christ. President Benson tried to drum that message into our consciousness and into our conduct during his entire tenure as president of the Church.

We are not directed to read the Book of Mormon primarily to learn history or geography or politics or ethics or culture or social or educational policy, though it contains valuable teachings on all those subjects. President Benson had teachings on many of those subjects, but he stressed one vital idea above all others: "All truths are not of the same value," he said. "The saving truths of salvation are of greatest worth."[14] He also said, "The Book of Mormon was written for us today. . . . The purpose of the Book of Mormon is stated on the title page. It is 'to the convincing of the Jew and Gentile that Jesus is the Christ, the Eternal God.' "[15]

We can see why President Benson emphasized the Book of Mormon's witness of Christ if we note carefully what is said to the Church in the verses from the eighty-fourth section of the Doctrine and Covenants President Benson quoted so frequently. In the verses preceding the quote, the Lord commanded the early Saints to heed the words of eternal life and to live by every word that proceeded forth from the mouth of God. He told them that those who came unto God would be taught "of the covenant which he has renewed and confirmed upon you . . . for the sake of the whole world" (D&C 84:48). Then He explained that their minds had been "darkened because of unbelief" and because they had "treated lightly the things [they had] received." The Lord explained that this had "brought the whole church under condemnation" (D&C 84:54–55). Then, in the quoted verse, He declared:

"And they shall remain under this condemnation until they repent and remember the new covenant, even the Book of Mormon and the former commandments which I have given them, not only to say, but to do according to that which I have written" (D&C 84:57).

This revelation states that the condemnation can be removed by repenting and remembering "the new covenant." What is this "new covenant, even the Book of Mormon and the former commandments which I have given them" (D&C 84:57)?

This covenant is obviously inseparable from the Book of Mormon, as has frequently been said, but it also includes "the former commandments" that the Lord had given His people.

I believe this "new covenant" mentioned in verse 57 is the same as "the covenant" described in verse 48, which the Father teaches and "has renewed and confirmed upon" those who come unto him, all "for the sake of the whole world." Under this interpretation, the "new covenant," whose neglect the Lord condemned, was the covenant contained in the Book of Mormon and in the "former commandments" the Lord had now renewed and confirmed upon the early Saints. These former commandments must have been the Lord's prior revelations, as contained in the Bible (the Old and New Testaments) and in those modern revelations already given to the Saints.[16]

The fundamental doctrinal nature of this "new covenant" the Saints had "treated lightly" is suggested by the two other revelations that mention "the new covenant." Both of these refer to

Jesus Christ as "the mediator of the new covenant" (D&C 76:69; 107:19; Hebrews 12:24).

This "new covenant" is frequently mentioned in the scriptures, ancient and modern. Jeremiah prophesied a "new covenant with the house of Israel" (Jeremiah 31:31; Hebrews 8:8). The New Testament teaches that Christ was "the mediator of a better covenant, which was established upon better promises" (Hebrews 8:6). The Prophet Joseph Smith declared that this covenant was not put in force at the time of Christ's mortal ministry because Israel rejected Him.[17] In a revelation given the same month the restored Church was organized, the Lord declared, "I say unto you that all old covenants have I caused to be done away in this thing; and this is a new and an everlasting covenant, even that which was from the beginning" (D&C 22:1).

The covenant described in these scriptures, made new by its renewal and confirmation in these latter days, refers to our covenant relationship with Jesus Christ. It incorporates the fullness of the gospel (D&C 66:2, 132:6), which President Joseph Fielding Smith described as "the sum total of all gospel covenants and obligations."[18] From the foregoing it is evident that the "new covenant" contained in the Book of Mormon and the former commandments is that central promise of the gospel, rooted in the atonement and resurrection of Jesus Christ. That promise gives us the assurance of immortality and the opportunity for eternal life if we will repent of our sins and make and keep the gospel covenant with our Savior. By this means, and through His grace, we can realize the great promise "that through the Atonement of Christ, all mankind may be saved, by obedience to the laws and ordinances of the Gospel" (Articles of Faith 1:3).

Thus, the "new covenant," the "new and everlasting covenant" the early Saints had received and treated lightly by the time the quoted revelation was given, included all of the commandments and ordinances of the gospel, which are explained most clearly (but not exclusively) in the Book of Mormon. As President

Benson said, "When used together, the Bible and the Book of Mormon confound false doctrines."[19] The Book of Mormon is "Another Testament of Jesus Christ." Its title page identifies its purpose, to explain "the covenants of the Lord" and to convince Jew and Gentile "that Jesus is the Christ, the Eternal God."

In declaring how the Saints could be relieved of condemnation for unbelief and for treating this new covenant lightly, the Lord emphasized that the new covenant requires positive action, not just passive commitment. In an inspired statement about temple covenants, Elder John A. Widtsoe explained that a covenant "is merely a promise to give life to knowledge, by making knowledge useful and helpful in man's daily progress. . . . The covenant gives life to truth, and makes possible the blessings that reward all those who use knowledge properly."[20]

This explains why the revelation requires us to "repent and remember the new covenant . . . not only to say, but to do according to that which I have written" (D&C 84:57). In short, in order to escape condemnation, we must come unto Christ and enter into the gospel covenant, not only "to say" but also "to do according to that which [the Lord has] written." We must "give diligent heed to the words of eternal life" and "live by every word that proceedeth forth from the mouth of God" (D&C 84:43–44).

We can easily see things in our own day that could cause the Lord to call us to "repent and remember the new covenant" and cause His prophet to declare that the Lord's condemnation has not yet been lifted. In our time we are seeing a great increase in the visibility and influence of those who deny or doubt the divinity of Jesus Christ and the need for His atonement.

Noting this trend many years ago, President Harold B. Lee declared: "Now . . . our greatest responsibility and anxiety is to defend the divine mission of our Lord and Master, Jesus Christ, for all about us, even among those who claim to be professors of the Christian faith, are those not willing to stand squarely in defense of the great truth that our Lord and Master, Jesus Christ, was indeed the Son of God. So tonight it would seem to me that the most important thing I could say to you is to try to strengthen your faith and increase your courage and your understanding of the place of the Master in the great Plan of Salvation."[21]

One of the principal reasons our Heavenly Father had President Benson direct us into a more intensive study of the Book of Mormon is to help us counteract this modern tendency to try to diminish the divinity and mission of our Savior. Are we as Latter-day Saints doing what we should to counteract this modern trend? Are we aware that our knowledge and testimony of the literal divinity, resurrection, and atonement of Jesus Christ are more distinctive and more needed with each passing year?

I suggest that many Latter-day Saints are not yet aware of our unique position and our special responsibilities to testify of Christ. I suggest that we are not yet doing all we should. I believe this is a sufficient explanation for the condemnation President Benson described and the call to repentance he issued. Here are some illustrations.

I believe that for a time and until recently our public talks and our literature were deficient in the frequency and depth with which they explained and rejoiced in those doctrinal subjects most closely related to the atonement of the Savior. A prominent gospel scholar saw this deficiency in our church periodicals published in a twenty-three year period ending in 1983.[22] I saw this same deficiency when I reviewed the subjects of general conference addresses during the decade ending in the mid-1980s.

Another illustration is provided by some Latter-day Saint funerals. I attend some funerals and hear reports of many others. Worthy tributes to the deceased are appropriate and so are family memories. But such matters must not dominate an LDS funeral service to the exclusion or neglect of those gospel truths that review the purpose of life and testify of our Creator and Redeemer. At a funeral service—of all places—we must not neglect to testify of Him whose gospel gives meaning and purpose to life and whose resurrection and atonement give hope for the deceased and comfort to the bereaved. Yet, I know of some LDS funerals in which no mention of the resurrection or the Savior was made. Is not this an example of "treat[ing] lightly the things [we] have received"? Is not this another cause for some of us to "repent and remember the new covenant"?

It is also possible for us to neglect "the new covenant" and to treat the gospel lightly in the daily activities of our lives. Salvation is in Christ, not in most things that occupy our time. All of our important and interesting debates about sports, fashion, entertainment personalities, and the like are insignificant by comparison with this. All of our efforts for the "good life," desirable as they are, are not sufficient for the salvation that is exaltation.

Have we "treated lightly the things [we] have received"? If we have, we need to "repent and remember the new covenant" (D&C 84:54, 57), putting the Savior uppermost in our minds and hearts, and showing a higher level of concern for His gospel, His commandments, His Sabbath, His work.

Fortunately, we are doing better. For at least two decades we have more consciously and more effectively presented ourselves in our true light as followers and servants of Jesus Christ. In 1982, the First Presidency and Quorum of the Twelve reminded us on the title page of the Book of Mormon that this great book is "Another Testament of Jesus Christ."

The First Presidency has repeatedly requested that we not refer to ourselves as "The Mormon Church" but by the name the Lord gave His Church by revelation: "The Church of Jesus Christ of Latter-day Saints" (D&C 115:4). On January 1, 2000, as part of the Church's observance of the new millennium, the First Presidency and Quorum of the Twelve issued a "Testimony of the Apostles," titled "The Living Christ." That year the Church also produced a videotape, *Special Witnesses of Christ*, which presented the personal testimonies of fifteen living apostles.

A statement by the General Presidency of the Relief Society, presented at the general Relief Society meeting in September 1999, identified the organization's "worldwide sisterhood" as "united in [their] devotion to Jesus Christ, our Savior and Exemplar," and as women of faith who "increase our testimonies of Jesus Christ through prayer and scripture study."[23]

Our Young Women theme uses a familiar Book of Mormon scripture to pledge that daughters of our Heavenly Father will "stand as witnesses of God at all times and in all things, and in all places" (Mosiah 18:9).

Recent LDS gospel scholarship clearly shows a greatly increased emphasis on the Savior and His atonement. Elder Bruce R. McConkie's multivolume work on the Messiah (1978–82) and his earlier three-volume *New Testament Commentary* (1965–73) are illustrative of this effort. So is Elder Jeffrey R. Holland's volume *Christ and the New Covenant* (1997). We have all benefited immeasurably from the BYU Religious Studies Center's annual Book of Mormon Symposia, which have placed appropriate emphasis on this scripture's preeminent position as a witness of Christ. Individual Latter-day Saint scholars, principally in religious instruction at Brigham Young University, have published brilliant and inspired books that have made important additions to our literature on the Savior and His atonement.[24] I hope such books are read and pondered, not just purchased and possessed.

President Benson's emphasis on reading and rereading the Book of Mormon is a heaven-sent refining of emphasis in the lives and gospel study of individual members of the Church. His challenge, reiterated by President Gordon B. Hinckley, has been accepted by multitudes of Latter-day Saints and is blessing lives everywhere.

Today, our General Authorities, auxiliary officers, and local leaders give more frequent and more in-depth attention to our sacred mission of testifying of Christ and of explaining the doctrines of His atonement. Our fine seminary and institute teachers have likewise been inspired to more effective teaching and witnessing of the Savior. As a result of President Benson's teachings, all Latter-day Saints are more conscious of the vital importance of the Book of Mormon in this effort. We are more aware of our duty and privilege to use this book to testify of Christ and to explain the new covenant—the principles and covenants of His gospel.

Our Church leaders and scholars have identified important facts we can use in this effort. For example, the word atonement appears only once in the entire New Testament, but it appears twenty-eight times in the Book of Mormon. The Book of Mormon is clearly the most profound treatment of this supremely important subject found anywhere.[25] The Book of Mormon has nearly one hundred names for the Savior, each expressing some nuance of meaning that enriches our understanding of His divine nature and mission.[26] Finally, as President Benson noted in one of his conference talks, "Over one-half of all the verses in the Book of Mormon refer to our Lord. Some form of Christ's name is mentioned more frequently per verse in the Book of Mormon than even in the New Testament."[27]

Fortunately, many God-fearing Christians still join us in testifying of the divinity and mission of Jesus Christ. For some years I have enjoyed sharing one such testimony. In many ways it is a model for Latter-day Saints, who have a duty to testify of Christ. These are the words of the late Malcolm Muggeridge, British author, journalist and television commentator.

"I may, I suppose, regard myself, or pass for being, a relatively successful man. People occasionally stare at me in the streets—that's fame. I can fairly easily earn enough to qualify for admission to the higher slopes of the Internal Revenue—that's success. Furnished with money and a little fame even the elderly, if they care to, may partake of trendy diversions—that's pleasure. It might happen once in a while that something I said or wrote was sufficiently heeded for me to persuade myself that it represented a serious impact on our time—that's fulfillment. Yet I say to you—

and I beg you to believe me—multiply these tiny triumphs by a million, add them all together, and they are nothing—less than nothing, a positive imperilment—measured against one draught of that living water Christ offers to the spiritually thirsty, irrespective of who or what they are."[28]

Men and women unquestionably have impressive powers and can bring to pass great things. But after all our obedience and good works, we cannot be saved from death or the effects of our individual sins without the grace extended by the atonement of Jesus Christ. The Book of Mormon makes this clear. It teaches that "salvation doth not come by the law alone" (Mosiah 13:28). In other words, salvation does not come simply by keeping the commandments. "By the law no flesh is justified" (2 Nephi 2:5). Even those who try to obey and serve God with all their heart, might, mind, and strength are unprofitable servants (Mosiah 2:21). Man cannot earn his own salvation. He cannot be cleansed by personal suffering for his own sins.

The Book of Mormon teaches, "Since man had fallen he could not merit anything of himself" (Alma 22:14). "There can be nothing which is short of an infinite atonement which will suffice for the sins of the world" (Alma 34:12; 2 Nephi 9:7). "Wherefore, redemption cometh in and through the Holy Messiah; . . . He offereth himself a sacrifice for sin, to answer the ends of the law" (2 Nephi 2:6–7). Consequently, "there is no flesh that can dwell in the presence of God, save it be through the merits, and mercy, and grace of the Holy Messiah" (2 Nephi 2:8). And so we "rejoice in Christ, we preach of Christ, . . . that our children may know to what source they may look for a remission of their sins" (2 Nephi 25:26).

These teachings obviously stand in opposition to the belief or assumption of some mortals (perhaps even some members of our Church) that they have no need of Christ because they can save themselves by their own works. As members of The Church of Jesus Christ of Latter-day Saints, we testify with the Book of

Mormon prophet-king Benjamin that "there shall be no other name given nor any other way nor means whereby salvation can come unto the children of men, only in and through the name of Christ, the Lord Omnipotent. For behold . . . salvation was, and is, and is to come, in and through the atoning blood of Christ" (Mosiah 3:17–18).

And so we say to all, in the words the prophet Moroni wrote as a conclusion to the Book of Mormon: "Come unto Christ, and be perfected in him; and deny yourselves of all ungodliness; and if ye shall deny yourselves of all ungodliness, and love God with all your might, mind and strength, then is his grace sufficient for you, that by his grace ye may be perfect in Christ. . . .

"And again, if ye by the grace of God are perfect in Christ, and deny not his power, then are ye sanctified in Christ by the grace of God, through the shedding of the blood of Christ, which is in the covenant of the Father unto the remission of your sins, that ye become holy, without spot" (Moroni 10:32–33).

This is the new covenant, as explained in the Book of Mormon. May we follow the commandment to give diligent heed to these words of eternal life, that we may remove the condemnation that comes from treating this new covenant lightly.

From an address delivered at Brigham Young University on June 6, 1993, and published in the Ensign, *March 1994, 60–67.*

NOTES

1. "A Sacred Responsibility," *Ensign,* May 1986, 78; almost all of President Benson's words quoted herein are also found in his book, *A Witness and a Warning,* published in 1988 by Deseret Book.
2. "Joseph Smith: Prophet to Our Generation," *Ensign,* November 1981, 61.
3. "'Come Unto Christ,'" *Ensign,* November 1987, 83.
4. "The Book of Mormon Is the Word of God," *Ensign,* May 1975, 65.
5. *History of The Church of Jesus Christ of Latter-day Saints,* ed. B. H. Roberts, 2d ed. rev., 7 vols., Salt Lake City: The Church of Jesus Christ of Latter-day Saints, 1932–51, 4:461.

6. "The Book of Mormon—Keystone of Our Religion," *Ensign,* November 1986, 5–6.
7. *History of the Church,* 4:461.
8. "The Book of Mormon—Keystone of Our Religion," 6, 5.
9. "The Book of Mormon—Keystone of Our Religion," 4.
10. "The Book of Mormon—Keystone of our Religion," 7.
11. "A New Witness for Christ," *Ensign,* November 1984, 6.
12. "The Book of Mormon Is the Word of God," *Ensign,* January 1988, 3, 4.
13. "'Come Unto Christ,'" 85.
14. "Worthy Fathers, Worthy Sons," *Ensign,* November 1985, 36.
15. "The Book of Mormon Is the Word of God," *Ensign,* January 1988, 3.
16. *History of the Church,* 1:318, 320.
17. *Teachings of the Prophet Joseph Smith,* sel. Joseph Fielding Smith, Salt Lake City: Deseret Book, 1976, 14–15.
18. *Doctrines of Salvation,* comp. Bruce R. McConkie, 3 vols., Salt Lake City: Bookcraft, 1954–66, 1:156.
19. "A New Witness for Christ," *Ensign,* November 1984, 8.
20. Assembly Hall Lecture, 12 October 1920; reprinted in *Best Loved Talks of the LDS People,* ed. Jay M. Parry et al., Salt Lake City: Deseret Book, 2002, 482.
21. Quoted in Robert J. Matthews, "What the Book of Mormon Tells Us About Jesus Christ," in *The Book of Mormon: The Keystone Scripture,* Provo, Utah: Religious Studies Center, 1988, 23.
22. Daniel H. Ludlow observation, cited in Bruce C. Hafen, *The Broken Heart,* Salt Lake City: Deseret Book, 1989, 3–4.
23. Mary Ellen Smoot, "Rejoice, Daughters of Zion," *Ensign,* November 1999, 92.
24. Stephen E. Robinson, *Believing Christ* (Deseret Book, 1992); Robert L. Millet, *Life in Christ* (Bookcraft, 1990); Bruce C. Hafen, *The Broken Heart* (Deseret Book, 1989); Robert J. Matthews, *Behold the Messiah* (Bookcraft, 1994).
25. Boyd K. Packer, "Atonement, Agency, Accountability," *Ensign,* May 1988, 69–70.
26. "What the Book of Mormon Tells Us About Jesus Christ," 32–33.
27. "'Come Unto Christ,'" 83; also see Matthews, 33.
28. *Jesus Rediscovered,* Garden City, N.Y.: Doubleday, 1969, 61.

9

TAKING UPON US THE NAME OF JESUS CHRIST

MEMBERS OF THE CHURCH OF Jesus Christ of Latter-day Saints are commanded to partake of the sacrament each week (D&C 59:9, 12). In doing so, they "witness" unto God the Eternal Father, as stated in the prayer on the bread, that they are "willing to take upon them the name of thy Son, and always remember him and keep his commandments which he has given them" (D&C 20:77; Moroni 4:3). We should ponder these sacred covenants during the sacrament service.

I wish to focus on the first of the solemn witnesses we make in partaking of the sacrament: that we are willing to take upon us the name of the Son of God the Eternal Father. Our witness that we are willing to take upon us the name of Jesus Christ has several meanings. Some of these meanings are obvious and well within the understanding of children. Others are only evident to those who have searched the scriptures and pondered the wonders of eternal life.

One of the obvious meanings renews a promise we made when we were baptized. Following the scriptural pattern, persons who are baptized "witness before the church that they have truly repented of all their sins and are willing to take upon them the name of Jesus Christ, having a determination to serve him to the end" (D&C 20:37; 2 Nephi 31:13; Moroni 6:3). When we partake of the sacrament, we renew this covenant and all the other covenants we made in the waters of baptism.[1]

As a second obvious meaning, we take upon us our Savior's name when we become members of The Church of Jesus Christ of Latter-day Saints. By His commandment, this church bears His name (D&C 115:4; 3 Nephi 27:7–8). Every member, young and old, is a member of the "household of God" (Ephesians 2:19). As true believers in Christ, as Christians, we have gladly taken His name upon us (Alma 46:15). As King Benjamin taught his people, "Because of the covenant which ye have made ye shall be called the children of Christ, his sons, and his daughters; for behold, this day he hath spiritually begotten you" (Mosiah 5:7; Alma 5:14; Alma 36:23–26).

We also take upon us the name of Jesus Christ whenever we publicly proclaim our belief in Him. Each of us has many opportunities to proclaim our belief to friends and neighbors, fellow workers, and casual acquaintances. As the Apostle Peter taught the Saints of his day, we should "sanctify the Lord God in [our] hearts: and be ready always to give an answer to every man that asketh [us] a reason of the hope that is in [us]" (1 Peter 3:15). In this way, we keep the modern commandment: "Take upon you the name of Christ, and speak the truth in soberness" (D&C 18:21).

A third meaning appeals to the understanding of those mature enough to know that a follower of Christ is obligated to serve Him. Many scriptural references to the name of the Lord seem to be references to the work of His kingdom. Thus, when Peter and the other apostles were beaten, they rejoiced "that they were counted worthy to suffer shame for his name" (Acts 5:41).

Paul wrote to certain members who had ministered to the Saints that the Lord would not forget the labor of love they had "shewed toward his name" (Hebrews 6:10). According to this meaning, by witnessing our willingness to take upon us the name of Jesus Christ, we signify our willingness to do the work of His kingdom.

In these three relatively obvious meanings, we see that we take upon us the name of Christ when we are baptized in His name, when we belong to His Church and profess our belief in Him, and when we do the work of His kingdom.

More mature members of the Church should understand and ponder other, deeper meanings as they partake of the sacrament. It is significant that when we partake of the sacrament we do not witness that we *take upon us* the name of Jesus Christ. We witness that we are *willing* to do so (D&C 20:77). The fact that we only witness to our willingness suggests that something else must happen before we actually take that sacred name upon us in the most important sense.

What future event or events could this covenant contemplate? The scriptures suggest two sacred possibilities, one concerning the authority of God, especially as exercised in the temples, and the other—closely related—concerning exaltation in the celestial kingdom.

The name of God is sacred. The Lord's Prayer begins with the words, "Our Father which art in heaven, Hallowed be thy name" (Matthew 6:9). From Sinai came the commandment, "Thou shalt not take the name of the Lord thy God in vain" (Exodus 20:7; Deuteronomy 5:11). Latter-day revelation equates this with using the name of God without authority. "Let all men beware how they take my name in their lips," the Lord declares in a modern revelation, for "many there be who . . . use the name of the Lord, and use it in vain, having not authority" (D&C 63:61–62).

Consistent with these references, many scriptures that refer to "the name of Jesus Christ" obviously refer to the authority of the Savior. This was surely the meaning conveyed when the seventy reported to Jesus that "even the devils are subject unto us through thy name" (Luke 10:17). The Doctrine and Covenants employs this same meaning when it describes the Twelve Apostles of this dispensation as "they who shall desire to take upon them my name with full purpose of heart" (D&C 18:27). The Twelve were later designated as "special witnesses of the name of Christ in all the world," and as those who "officiate in the name of the Lord, under the direction of the Presidency of the Church" (D&C 107:23, 33).

By way of further illustration, the Old Testament contains scores of references to the name of the Lord in a context that clearly means the authority of the Lord. Most of these references have to do with the temple.

When the children of Israel had not yet crossed the Jordan, the Lord told them that when they entered the promised land there should be a place where the Lord their God would "cause his name to dwell" (Deuteronomy 12:11; 14:23–24; 16:6). Time after time in succeeding revelations, the Lord and His servants referred to the future temple as a house for "the name" of the Lord God of Israel (1 Kings 3:2; 5:5; 8:16–20, 29, 44, 48; 1 Chronicles 22:8–10, 19; 29:16; 2 Chronicles 2:4; 6:5–10, 20, 34, 38). After the temple was dedicated, the Lord appeared to tell Solomon that He had hallowed the temple "to put my name there for ever" (1 Kings 9:3; 2 Chronicles 7:16).

Similarly, in modern revelation the Lord refers to temples as houses built "unto my holy name" (D&C 124:39; 105:33; 109:2–5). In the inspired dedicatory prayer of the Kirtland Temple, the Prophet Joseph Smith asked the Lord for a blessing upon "thy people upon whom thy name shall be put in this house" (D&C 109:26).

All of these references to ancient and modern temples as houses for "the name" of the Lord obviously involve something far more significant than a mere inscription of His sacred name on the structure. The scriptures speak of the Lord's putting His name in a temple because He gives authority for His name to be used in the sacred ordinances of that house. That is one meaning of the Prophet's reference to the Lord's putting His name upon His people in that holy house (D&C 109:26).

Willingness to take upon us the name of Jesus Christ can therefore be understood as willingness to take upon us the authority of Jesus Christ. According to this meaning, by partaking of the sacrament we witness our willingness to participate in the sacred ordinances of the temple and to receive the highest blessings available through the name and by the authority of the Savior when He chooses to confer them upon us.

Another future event we may anticipate when we witness our willingness to take that sacred name upon us concerns our relationship to our Savior and the incomprehensible blessings available to those who will be called by His name at the last day.

King Benjamin told his people, "There shall be no other name given nor any other way nor means whereby salvation can come unto the children of men, only in and through the name of Christ, the Lord Omnipotent" (Mosiah 3:17; 2 Nephi 31:21). Peter proclaimed "the name of Jesus Christ of Nazareth" to the leaders of the Jews, declaring that "there is none other name under heaven given among men, whereby we must be saved" (Acts 4:10, 12; D&C 18:21).

The scriptures proclaim that the Savior's atoning sacrifice was for those who "believe on his name." Alma taught that Jesus Christ, the Son, the Only Begotten of the Father, would come "to take away the sins of the world, yea, the sins of every man who steadfastly believeth on his name" (Alma 5:48; 9:27; 11:40; Helaman 14:2). In the words of King Benjamin, "Whosoever doeth this shall be found at the right hand of God, for he shall know the name by which he is called; for he shall be called by the name of Christ" (Mosiah 5:9).

Thus, those who exercise faith in the sacred name of Jesus Christ, repent of their sins, enter into His covenant, and keep His commandments (Mosiah 5:8) can lay claim on the atoning sacrifice of Jesus Christ. Those who do so will be called by His name at the last day.

When the Savior taught the Nephites following His resurrection, He referred to the scriptural statement that "ye must take upon you the name of Christ." He explained, "For by this name shall ye be called at the last day; and whoso taketh upon him my name, and endureth to the end, the same shall be saved at the last day" (3 Nephi 27:5–6). This same teaching is repeated in a modern revelation, which adds the caution that "if they know not the name by which they are called, they cannot have place in the kingdom of my Father" (D&C 18:25; Alma 5:38).

The Book of Mormon explains the significance of being called by the name of Jesus Christ. When the Savior showed His spirit body to the brother of Jared, He introduced Himself as the Father and the Son, declaring that through His redeeming sacrifice all mankind who believe on His name should have life eternal through Him, "and they shall become my sons and my daughters" (Ether 3:14).

The prophet Abinadi said that those who believe in the Lord and look to Him for a remission of their sins "are his seed, or they are the heirs of the kingdom of God. For these are they whose sins he has borne; these are they for whom he has died, to redeem them from their transgressions. And now, are they not his seed?" (Mosiah 15:11–12).

Speaking through the prophet Alma the Elder, the Lord explained the significance of this relationship: "For behold, in my name are they called; and if they know me they shall come forth, and shall have a place eternally at my right hand" (Mosiah 26:24).

In these great scriptures from the Book of Mormon, we learn that those who qualify by faith, repentance, and compliance with the laws and ordinances of the gospel will have their sins borne by the Lord Jesus Christ. In spiritual and figurative terms they will become the sons and daughters of Christ, heirs to His kingdom. These are they who will be called by His name in the last day.

According to this meaning, when we witness our *willingness* to take upon us the name of Jesus Christ, we are signifying our commitment to do all we can to achieve eternal life in the kingdom of our Father. We are expressing our candidacy for—our determination to strive for—exaltation in the celestial kingdom.

Those who are found worthy to take upon them the name of Jesus Christ at the last day are described in the great revelations recorded in the ninety-third and seventy-sixth sections of the Doctrine and Covenants. In these revelations, the Savior made known to Joseph Smith that in due time, if we keep the commandments of God, we can receive the "fulness" of the Father (D&C 93:19–20). Here, the Savior bears record that "all those who are begotten through me are partakers of the glory of the [Father], and are the church of the Firstborn" (D&C 93:22). "They are they into whose hands the Father has given all things. . . . Wherefore, as it is written, they are gods" who "shall dwell in the presence of God and his Christ forever and ever" (D&C 76:55, 58, 62). "And this is life eternal, that they might know thee the only true God, and Jesus Christ, whom thou hast sent" (John 17:3; D&C 88:4–5).

This is the ultimate significance of taking upon us the name of Jesus Christ, and this is what we should ponder as we partake of the sacred emblems of the sacrament. As we do so, we glory in the mission of the risen Lord, who lived and taught and suffered and died and rose again that all mankind might have immortality *and eternal life.*

From an address published in the Ensign, *May 1985, 80–83.*

NOTE

1. Joseph Fielding Smith, *Doctrines of Salvation,* comp. Bruce R. McConkie, 3 vols., Salt Lake City: Bookcraft, 1954–56, 2:341, 346.

10

ALWAYS REMEMBER HIM

In April 1830 the Lord commanded the members of His newly restored Church to "meet together often to partake of bread and wine in the remembrance of the Lord Jesus" (D&C 20:75). This was the same instruction He gave when He introduced this ordinance nearly two thousand years ago: "And he took bread, and gave thanks, and brake it, and gave unto them, saying, This is my body which is given for you: this do in remembrance of me" (Luke 22:19).

When we partake of the sacrament, we witness unto God the Eternal Father that we "do always remember" His Son (D&C 20:77, 79; 3 Nephi 18:7, 11). Each Sabbath day millions of Latter-day Saints make this promise. What does it mean to "always remember" our Savior?

To remember means to keep in memory. In the scriptures, to remember often means to keep a person in memory, together with associated emotions like love, loyalty, and gratitude. The stronger the emotion, the more vivid and influential the memory. Here are some examples:

1. Most of us have clear memories of our mortal parents, who gave us birth and nurtured us through childhood. These kinds of memories do not dim with the passing years but with wisdom and perspective become ever more meaningful. As I grow older, I think more frequently of my father and my mother. I will always remember them.

2. Shortly before my wife was to give birth to our first child, we learned that the baby had to be born by cesarean section. I was then a student at Brigham Young University, going to school full time and working almost full time. From my meager earnings, a little more than one dollar an hour, we had saved enough money for the hospital and doctor bills, but nothing in our plans or emotions had prepared us for this shocking announcement. We scarcely knew what a cesarean birth was, and we feared the worst.

A few days later we faced our ordeal. After what seemed an eternity, I stood at a window in the hospital hallway, looking into a basket containing our firstborn. The joy of seeing our daughter and knowing that my beloved companion had survived the operation was inexpressible. As I experienced that moment, I became aware of a stranger standing beside me. He introduced himself as Dr. N. Frederick Hicken, the surgeon who had come from Salt Lake City to perform the operation. His presence reminded me that a surgeon's fee had not been in our plans, and I began to ask him if I could pay his fee over a period of time.

"Don't worry about that, young man," he said in a kindly way. "This is one from the Hickens to the Oakses." Before I could stammer a thank-you, he was gone.

I was filled with wonder at this unexpected gift. Our benefactor must have known my father, a young medical doctor who died when I was a boy. He must have given us this gift because of something my father had done. I marveled at the goodness of this man who had come to us in our crisis and had, without recompense, used his powers to preserve the lives of those I loved. The emotion of that moment made the memory indelible. The name of that doctor is precious to me. I will always remember him.

3. Some time ago, someone praised me for something I had done. Even as I received that compliment I knew I did not deserve it. The credit belonged to wise and wonderful teachers who had taught me what to do and how to do it. My teachers were memorable. I shudder to think what I would have lost if teachers had not helped me want to learn and then taught me what I needed to know. I will always be grateful to my teachers. I will always remember them.

The reasons that I will always remember these persons are related to the reasons that we should always remember Jesus Christ: He is our Creator, our Redeemer, and our Teacher.

Under the direction and according to the plan of God the Father, His Son, Jehovah, "created the heavens and the earth, and all things that in them are" (3 Nephi 9:15). The Son gave us life in the beginning of this world, and through the power of His resurrection He will give each of us life again after we have died in mortality.

He is our Redeemer. According to the Father's plan, He provided the atoning sacrifice that can rescue us from the extremity of spiritual death. As a freewill offering, the Only Begotten Son of God came to earth and shed His blood for the remission of our sins (D&C 27:2).

Our Creator and our Redeemer is also our teacher. He taught us how to live. He gave us commandments, and if we follow them, we will receive blessings and happiness in this world and eternal life in the world to come.

And so we see that He whom we should always remember is He who gave us mortal life, showed us the way to a happy life, and redeemed us so we can have immortality and eternal life.

If we keep our covenant to "always remember him," we can

"always have his spirit to be with [us]" (D&C 20:77, 79). That spirit will testify of Him, and it will guide us unto truth.

The Son's teachings and example will guide and strengthen us in the way we should live. The process was described in the words of a once-popular song: "Try to remember, and if you remember, then follow."[1]

I will now refer to some of His teachings we should remember and follow.

Follow is the word the Savior used when He called His helpers to the ministry. As He was walking by the Sea of Galilee, He saw two fishermen, Simon Peter and his brother, Andrew, at work in their vocation. "And he saith unto them, Follow me, and I will make you fishers of men" (Matthew 4:19). "And straightway they forsook their nets, and followed him" (Mark 1:18).

Here the Savior established a pattern for those He calls to do His work. Acting through His servants, for He has said that "by mine own voice or by the voice of my servants, it is the same" (D&C 1:38), He calls us to take time from our daily activities to follow Him and serve our fellowmen. Even the greatest among us should be the "servant of all" (Mark 10:43–44). Those who always remember Him will straightway assume and faithfully fulfill the responsibilities to which they are called by His servants.

Among the teachings of our Savior that we should remember is that there are things about our fellowmen that we should forgive—the wrongs they have done to us. "Lord," the Apostle Peter asked the Master, "how oft shall my brother sin against me, and I forgive him? till seven times?" (Matthew 18:21). In response, Jesus taught the parable of the unforgiving servant. This servant owed a large debt to his king. When he begged for mercy, the king was moved with compassion and forgave the debt. But when a fellow servant owed him a debt, this man took his debtor by the throat and cast him into prison. When the unforgiving servant was brought to judgment, the king said:

"Shouldest not thou also have had compassion on thy

fellowservant, even as I had pity on thee? And his lord was wroth, and delivered him to the tormentors, till he should pay all that was due unto him. So likewise shall my heavenly Father do also unto you," (Matthew 18:33–35; 6:14–15; 3 Nephi 13:14–15).

As the Lord has told us in modern revelation, "He that forgiveth not his brother his trespasses standeth condemned before the Lord; for there remaineth in him the greater sin" (D&C 64:9). If we always remember our Savior, we will forgive and erase grievances against those who have wronged us.

At the beginning of His ministry, Jesus sought out John the Baptist, who was preaching "the baptism of repentance for the remission of sins" (Mark 1:4).

"Then cometh Jesus from Galilee to Jordan unto John, to be baptized of him. But John forbade him, saying, I have need to be baptized of thee, and comest thou to me? And Jesus answering said unto him, Suffer it to be so now: for thus it becometh us to fulfil all righteousness" (Matthew 3:13–15).

Those who seek to follow the Savior will understand the importance of the ordinance of baptism. The Lamb without blemish saw fit to submit Himself to baptism by one holding the authority of the priesthood in order to "fulfil all righteousness." How much more each of us has need of the cleansing and saving power of this ordinance and the other ordinances of the gospel.

As we always remember the Savior, we should strive to assure that we, our family members and, indeed, all sons and daughters of God everywhere follow Him into the waters of baptism. Remembering the Savior in this way reminds each of us of our duty to proclaim the gospel, perfect the Saints, and redeem the dead.

Remembering the Savior can also help us understand and endure the inevitable afflictions of this life. The Savior taught:

"Blessed are ye, when men shall revile you, and persecute you, and shall say all manner of evil against you falsely, for my sake. Rejoice, and be exceeding glad: for great is your reward in heaven:

for so persecuted they the prophets which were before you" (Matthew 5:11–12).

When the risen Lord appeared to the people in the ancient Americas, He taught them and called leaders to whom He gave the authority of His priesthood. Next He healed the sick, the lame, the blind, and all others who were afflicted in any manner. Then "he commanded that their little children should be brought" (3 Nephi 17:11). And He "blessed them, and prayed unto the Father for them" (3 Nephi 17:21).

As I remember this inspiring example, I remember visits and letters I have had from persons caring for loved ones who are sick or who are afflicted with the infirmities of old age. I also remember loved ones grieving over little children with life-shortening or crippling physical or emotional disabilities. How their hearts ache for their little ones! How they need our love and support! I also remember the words, "Inasmuch as ye have done it unto one of the least of these my brethren, ye have done it unto me" (Matthew 25:40). Here our Savior gives an assurance of blessings for those who carry such burdens, and He gives a challenge for others who lend them support.

We should always remember how the Savior taught us to love and do good to one another. Loving and serving one another can solve so many problems.

I remember receiving a letter from a sister in another country. She wrote about the plight of single adult members of the Church. "Where do I fit in?" she asked. She longed to join in her ward's social activities, but she said they were always designed for couples. She felt herself the "odd one out," forced by circumstances rather than choice to forego wholesome associations "rather than risk breaking up even numbers."

She also wrote of the trauma of being single as a result of divorce or of a companion's desertion or death. When she was a married woman, she said, "I never once gave much thought to the plight of the single sisters, except experiencing a kind of helpless pity for them." Now in that circumstance herself, she felt that the married sisters of her acquaintance tended to shun the sisters who were single. She asked me what could be done to help the single adult members of the Church with what she described as their "feelings of rejection, nonacceptance, and noncaring by their fellow Church members." Judging from the letters we receive, I believe there are many thousands of single adult members, our brothers and sisters, with similar feelings.

Our Savior gave us the parable of the good shepherd, who left the multitude and went in search of a single sheep who was lost (Luke 15:3–6). Does not that same principle require couples who enjoy loving companionship to go out of their way to include in their social circles brothers and sisters who have been deprived of that companionship? "Try to remember, and if you remember, then follow."

A few years ago I spoke by assignment to a chamber of commerce group in Salt Lake City. During a question-and-answer period, I listened to a fine woman who was not of our faith. She spoke movingly of the pain her children had experienced when they were shunned by LDS youth in school and social activities. More recently, a Utah convert to the Church wrote of his concern regarding the treatment received by some adults new to the state. They are of other faiths but come to Utah with good basic values and high expectations for a life among good neighbors and then, the convert wrote, "find themselves excluded at best and ostracized at worst."

Of course, there will be differences in the personal standards and social activities of faithful Latter-day Saints and members of other groups. But these differences are no excuse for ostracism, arrogance, or unkindness by LDS people. As my convert friend wrote, "I personally believe that Satan is as active among the Saints in turning them away from their neighbors as he is in turning disaffected persons against the Church."

As we covenant that we will always remember our Savior, we

must not forget Jehovah's command to Israel: "But the stranger that dwelleth with you shall be unto you as one born among you, and thou shalt love him as thyself" (Leviticus 19:34; Exodus 22:21; Deuteronomy 10:19).

We should always remember how Jesus commanded us to love our neighbor as ourselves. He illustrated that great teaching with the example of the Good Samaritan, who crossed the social barriers of his day to perform acts of kindness and mercy. Then the Savior said, "Go, and do thou likewise" (Luke 10:37).

While serving as the Lord's mouthpiece, President Spencer W. Kimball said, "Let us fellowship the students from all nations as they come to our land, so that we, above all other people, treat them as brothers and sisters in true friendship, whether or not they are interested in the gospel."[2]

That prophetic instruction should guide our relationships with all of our neighbors.

As we remember our Lord and Savior, we should contemplate the great blessings we have as members of The Church of Jesus Christ of Latter-day Saints. We have been taught by the Lord Jesus Christ. We have been led by His prophets. We have received the sealing ordinances of His gospel. He has blessed us bounteously.

As we contemplate these blessings, we should also remember the divine caution: "For of him unto whom much is given much is required" (D&C 82:3; Luke 12:48). That eternal principle of law and justice is a measure of what God expects of us. May we always remember it as we covenant to do.

From an address published in the Ensign, *May 1988, 29–32.*

Notes

1. Tom Jones and Harvey Schmidt, "Try to Remember," from *The Fantasticks,* New York: Chappell, 1960.
2. Regional Representatives' seminar, Salt Lake City, 29 September 1978.

11

ALWAYS HAVE
HIS SPIRIT

THERE IS A CLOSE RELATIONSHIP between our partaking of the sacrament and our enjoying the blessings available from the gift of the Holy Ghost. In modern revelation the Lord commands, "That thou mayest more fully keep thyself unspotted from the world, thou shalt go to the house of prayer and offer up thy sacraments upon my holy day" (D&C 59:9).

As we partake of the sacrament each week, we ponder the atonement of the Lord Jesus Christ and we reaffirm and renew the covenants we made when we were baptized. These acts of worship and commitment are described in the revealed prayer the priest offers upon the bread. As stated in that prayer, we partake of the bread "in remembrance of the body" of our Savior, and by doing so we witness to God, the Eternal Father, "that [we] are willing to take upon [us] the name of [His] Son, and always remember him and keep his commandments which he has given [us]" (D&C 20:77).

After we were baptized, hands were laid upon our heads and we were given the gift of the Holy Ghost. When we consciously and sincerely renew our baptismal covenants as we partake of the sacrament, we renew our qualification for the promise "that [we] may always have his Spirit to be with [us]" (D&C 20:77).

We cannot overstate the importance of that promise. President Wilford Woodruff called the gift of the Holy Ghost the greatest gift we can receive in mortality.[1] Unfortunately, the great value of that gift and the important conditions for its fulfillment are not well understood. Nephi prophesied that in the last days churches would be built up that would "teach with their learning, and deny the Holy Ghost, which giveth utterance" (2 Nephi 28:4). He pronounced "wo" upon "him that hearkeneth unto the precepts of men, and denieth the power of God, and the gift of the Holy Ghost!" (2 Nephi 28:26).

The Bible tells us that when the Savior gave His final instructions to His disciples, He promised that He would send them "the Comforter" (John 16:7). Earlier, He had taught them the mission of this comforter, which is otherwise referred to as the Holy Ghost, the Holy Spirit, the Spirit of the Lord, or simply the Spirit. That comforter dwells in us (John 14:17). He teaches us "all things and bring[s] all things to [our] remembrance" (John 14:26). He guides us into truth and shows us things to come (John 16:13). He testifies of the Son (John 15:26; 1 Corinthians 12:3). The Bible also teaches that the Savior and His servants will baptize "with the Holy Ghost, and with fire" (Matthew 3:11; Mark 1:8; John 1:33; Acts 1:5).

The Bible's teachings about the Holy Ghost are reaffirmed and elaborated in the Book of Mormon and in modern revelation. The Holy Ghost is the means by which God inspires and reveals His will to His children (D&C 8:2–3). The Holy Ghost bears record of the Father and of the Son (3 Nephi 28:11; D&C 20:27; 42:17). He enlightens our minds and fills us with joy (D&C 11:13). By the power of the Holy Ghost we "may know the truth of all things" (Moroni 10:5). By His power we may have the mysteries of God unfolded unto us (1 Nephi 10:19) and have all expedient things manifested unto us (D&C 18:18; D&C 39:6). The Holy Ghost shows us "all things what [we] should do" (2 Nephi 32:5). We teach the gospel as we are directed by the Holy Ghost, which carries our words into the hearts of those we teach (2 Nephi 33:1).

Latter-day scriptures also teach that the remission of sins, which is made possible by the Atonement, comes "by baptism, and by fire, yea, even the Holy Ghost" (D&C 19:31; 2 Nephi 31:17). Thus, the risen Lord pleaded with the Nephites to repent and come unto Him and be baptized, "that ye may be sanctified by the reception of the Holy Ghost, that ye may stand spotless before me at the last day" (3 Nephi 27:20).

The gift of the Holy Ghost is so important to our faith that a prophet gave it unique emphasis in a conversation with the president of the United States. Joseph Smith had journeyed to Washington, D.C., to seek help in recovering compensation for injuries and losses the Saints had suffered in the Missouri persecutions. In his meeting with President Martin Van Buren, Joseph was asked how the Church differed from the other religions of the day. The Prophet replied that "we differed in mode of baptism, and the gift of the Holy Ghost by the laying on of hands."[2] He later explained that he gave this answer because "all other considerations were contained in the gift of the Holy Ghost."[3]

In highlighting the gift of the Holy Ghost as a distinguishing characteristic of our faith, we need to understand the important differences between (1) the light of Christ, (2) a manifestation of the Holy Ghost, and (3) the gift of the Holy Ghost.

The light of Christ, which is sometimes called the spirit of Christ or the spirit of God, "giveth light to every man that cometh into the world" (D&C 84:46). This is the light "which is in all things, which giveth life to all things" (D&C 88:13). The prophet Mormon taught that "the Spirit of Christ is given to every man, that he may know good from evil" (Moroni 7:16; Moroni 7:19; 2 Nephi 2:5; Helaman 14:31). Elder Lorenzo Snow spoke of this light when he said, "Everybody has the Spirit of God."[4] The light of Christ enlightens and gives understanding to all men (D&C 88:11).

In contrast, a manifestation of the Holy Ghost is more focused. This manifestation is given to acquaint sincere seekers with the truth about the Lord and His gospel. For example, the prophet Moroni promises that when we study the Book of Mormon and seek to know whether it is true, sincerely and with real intent, God will "manifest the truth of it unto [us] by the power of the Holy Ghost" (Moroni 10:4). Moroni also records this promise from the risen Lord: "He that believeth these things which I have spoken, him will I visit with the manifestations of my Spirit, and he shall know and bear record. For because of my Spirit he shall know that these things are true" (Ether 4:11).

These manifestations are available to everyone. The Book of Mormon declares that the Savior "manifesteth himself unto all those who believe in him, by the power of the Holy Ghost; yea, unto every nation, kindred, tongue, and people" (2 Nephi 26:13).

To repeat, the light of Christ is given to all men and women that they may know good from evil; manifestations of the Holy Ghost are given to lead sincere seekers to gospel truths that will persuade them to repentance and baptism.

The gift of the Holy Ghost is more comprehensive. The Prophet Joseph Smith explained: "There is a difference between the Holy Ghost and the gift of the Holy Ghost. Cornelius received the Holy Ghost before he was baptized, which was the convincing power of God unto him of the truth of the Gospel, but he could not receive the *gift* of the Holy Ghost until after he was baptized. Had he not taken this sign or ordinance upon him, the Holy Ghost which convinced him of the truth of God, would have left him."[5]

The gift of the Holy Ghost includes the right to constant

companionship, that we may "always have his Spirit to be with [us]" (D&C 20:77). A newly baptized member told me what she felt when she received that gift. This was a faithful Christian woman who had spent her life in service to others. She knew and loved the Lord, and she had felt the manifestations of His spirit. When she received the added light of the restored gospel, she was baptized. The elders then placed their hands on her head and gave her the gift of the Holy Ghost. She recalled, "I felt the influence of the Holy Ghost settle upon me with greater intensity than I had ever felt before. He was like an old friend who had guided me in the past but now had come to stay."

For faithful members of the Church of Jesus Christ, the companionship of the Holy Spirit should be so familiar that they must use care not to take it for granted. For example, that good feeling we have while reading the scriptures or listening to inspired speakers or inspiring music is a confirming witness of the Spirit, available to faithful members on a continuing basis. A member once asked me why he felt so good about the talks and music in a sacrament meeting, while a guest he had invited that day apparently experienced no such feeling. This is but one illustration of the contrast between one who has the gift of the Holy Ghost and is in tune with its promptings and one who does not have the gift or is not in tune.

If we are practicing our faith and seeking the companionship of the Holy Spirit, we can feel the Spirit in our hearts and in our homes. Members of a family who have daily family prayer, seek to keep the commandments of God and honor His name, and speak lovingly to one another will have a spiritual feeling in their home that will be discernible to all who enter it. I know this because I have felt the presence or absence of that feeling in many LDS homes.

It is important to remember that the illumination and revelation that come to an individual as a result of the gift of the Holy Ghost do not come suddenly or without seeking. President Spencer W. Kimball taught that the Holy Ghost "comes a little at a time as you merit it. And as your life is in harmony, you gradually receive the Holy Ghost in a great measure."[6]

The blessings available through the gift of the Holy Ghost are conditioned upon worthiness. "The Spirit of the Lord doth not dwell in unholy temples" (Helaman 4:24; Mosiah 2:36–37; 1 Corinthians 3:16–17). Though we have a right to its constant companionship, the spirit of the Lord will dwell with us only when we keep the commandments. It will withdraw when we offend by profanity, uncleanliness, disobedience, rebellion, or other serious sins.

Worthy men and women who have the gift of the Holy Ghost can be edified and guided by inspiration and revelation. The Lord has declared that "the mysteries of his kingdom . . . are only to be seen and understood by the power of the Holy Spirit, which God bestows on those who love him, and purify themselves before him" (D&C 76:114, 116).

A few years ago I met with a prospective mission president and his wife to discuss their availability for service. I asked whether their responsibilities to aged parents would preclude their service at that time. This sister was the only daughter of a wonderful mother, then about eighty, whom she visited and helped each week. Though somewhat dependent physically, this mother was strong spiritually. She had served four missions and fifteen years as a temple worker. Because she was in tune with the Spirit, she had a remarkable experience.

Several months before this interview, this mother told her daughter that the Spirit had whispered that her daughter's husband would be called as a mission president. So advised, the mother had prepared herself for the needed separation and assured her daughter, long in advance of my assignment for the exploratory interview, that she would "not be a hindrance" to their service.

When we desire a remission of our sins through the atonement of our Savior, we are commanded to repent and come to

Him with a broken heart and a contrite spirit (3 Nephi 9:20; 12:19; Moroni 6:2; D&C 20:37). In the waters of baptism we witness to the Lord that we have repented of our sins and are willing to take His name upon us and "serve him to the end" (D&C 20:37).

Nephi described the effects of baptism: "For the gate by which ye should enter is repentance and baptism by water; and then cometh a remission of your sins by fire and by the Holy Ghost" (2 Nephi 31:17). That promise is fulfilled as a result of our receiving the gift of the Holy Ghost.

The need to keep our personal temple clean in order to have the companionship and guidance of the Holy Ghost explains the importance of the commandment to partake of the sacrament on the Sabbath. We should precede our partaking of the sacrament by repenting so that we come to this sacred ordinance with a broken heart and a contrite spirit (2 Nephi 2:7; 3 Nephi 12:19; D&C 59:8). Then, as we renew our baptismal covenants and affirm that we will "always remember him" (D&C 20:77), the Lord will renew the promised remission of our sins, under the conditions and at the time He chooses. One of the primary purposes and effects of this renewal of covenants and cleansing from sin is "that [we] may always have his Spirit to be with [us]" (D&C 20:77).

In view of these truths, all members of the Church, young and old, should attend sacrament meeting each Sabbath day and partake of the sacrament with the repentant attitude described as "a broken heart and a contrite spirit" (3 Nephi 9:20). The Savior has said that we should partake "with an eye single to my glory—remembering unto the Father my body which was laid down for you, and my blood which was shed for the remission of your sins" (D&C 27:2).

I pray that we will also partake of the sacrament with a submissive manner that will help us accept and serve in Church callings in order to comply with our solemn covenant to take His name and His work upon us. I also pray that we comply with our solemn covenant to keep His commandments.

To those brothers and sisters who may have allowed themselves to become lax in this vital renewal of the covenants of the sacrament, I plead in words of the First Presidency that you "come back and feast at the table of the Lord, and taste again the sweet and satisfying fruits of fellowship with the saints."[7] Let us qualify ourselves for our Savior's promise that by partaking of the sacrament we will "be filled" (3 Nephi 20:8; 18:9), which means that we will be "filled with the Spirit" (3 Nephi 20:9). That Spirit— the Holy Ghost—is our comforter, our direction finder, our communicator, our interpreter, our witness, and our purifier— our infallible guide and sanctifier for our mortal journey toward eternal life.

Any who may have thought it a small thing to partake of the sacrament should remember the Lord's declaration that the foundation of a great work is laid by small things, for "out of small things proceedeth that which is great" (D&C 64:33). Out of the seemingly small act of consciously and reverently renewing our baptismal covenants comes a renewal of the blessings of baptism by water and by the Spirit, that we may always have His Spirit to be with us. In this way all of us will be guided, and in this way all of us can be cleansed.

From an address published in the Ensign, *November 1996, 59–61.*

NOTES

1. *The Discourses of Wilford Woodruff,* ed. G. Homer Durham, Salt Lake City: Bookcraft, 1969, 5.
2. *History of The Church of Jesus Christ of Latter-day Saints,* ed. B. H. Roberts, 2d ed. rev., 7 vols., Salt Lake City: The Church of Jesus Christ of Latter-day Saints, 1932–51, 4:42.
3. *History of the Church,* 4:42.

4. In *Journal of Discourses,* 26 vols., London: Latter-day Saints' Book Depot, 1854–86, 14:304.

5. *Teachings of the Prophet Joseph Smith,* sel. Joseph Fielding Smith, Salt Lake City: Deseret Book, 1976, 199; emphasis added.

6. *Teachings of Spencer W. Kimball,* ed. Edward L. Kimball, Salt Lake City: Bookcraft, 1982, 114.

7. "An Invitation to Come Back," *Church News,* 22 December 1985, 3.

12

HAVE YOU BEEN SAVED?

WHAT DO WE ANSWER WHEN someone asks us, "Have you been saved?" This question, so common in the conversation of some Christians, can be puzzling to members of The Church of Jesus Christ of Latter-day Saints because it is not our usual way of speaking. We tend to speak of *saved,* or *salvation,* as a future event rather than something that has already been realized.

Good Christian people sometimes attach different meanings to some key gospel terms like *saved* or *salvation.* If we answer according to what our questioner probably means in asking if we have been "saved," our answer must be, "Yes." If we answer according to the various meanings Latter-day Saints attach to the terms *saved* or *salvation,* our response will be either "Yes," or "Yes, but with conditions."

As I understand what is meant by the good Christians who speak in these terms, we are "saved" when we sincerely declare or confess that we have accepted Jesus Christ as our personal Lord and Savior. This meaning relies on words the Apostle Paul taught the Christians of his day:

"If thou shalt confess with thy mouth the Lord Jesus, and shalt believe in thine heart that God hath raised him from the dead, thou shalt be saved. For with the heart man believeth unto righteousness; and with the mouth confession is made unto salvation" (Romans 10:9–10).

To Latter-day Saints, the words *saved* and *salvation* in this teaching signify a present covenant relationship with Jesus Christ in which we are assured salvation from the consequences of sin if we are obedient. Every sincere Latter-day Saint is "saved" according to this meaning. We have been converted to the restored gospel of Jesus Christ, we have experienced repentance and baptism, and we are renewing our covenants of baptism by partaking of the sacrament.

Latter-day Saints use the words *saved* and *salvation* in at least six different ways. According to some of these meanings, our salvation is assured—we are already saved. In others, salvation must be spoken of as a future event (1 Corinthians 5:5), or as conditioned upon a future event (Mark 13:13). But in all of these meanings, or kinds of salvation, salvation is in and through Jesus Christ.

1. First, all mortals have been saved from the permanence of death through the resurrection of Jesus Christ. "For as in Adam all die, even so in Christ shall all be made alive" (1 Corinthians 15:22).

2. As to salvation from sin and the consequences of sin, our answer to the question of whether we have been saved is, "Yes, but with conditions." Our third article of faith declares our belief: "We believe that through the Atonement of Christ, all mankind may be saved, by obedience to the laws and ordinances of the Gospel" (Articles of Faith 1:3).

Many Bible verses declare that Jesus came to take away the

sins of the world (John 1:29; Matthew 26:28). The New Testament frequently refers to the grace of God and to salvation by grace (John 1:17; Acts 15:11; Ephesians 2:8). But the Bible also has many specific commandments on personal behavior and many references to the importance of works (Matthew 5:16; Ephesians 2:10; James 2:14–17). In addition, the Savior taught that we must endure to the end in order to be saved (Matthew 10:22; Mark 13:13).

Relying upon the totality of Bible teachings and upon clarifications received through modern revelation, we testify that being cleansed from sin through Christ's atonement is conditioned upon our faith, which must be manifested by obedience to the Lord's command to repent, be baptized, and receive the Holy Ghost (Acts 2:37–38). "Verily, verily, I say unto thee," Jesus taught, "Except a man be born of water and of the Spirit, he cannot enter into the kingdom of God" (John 3:5; Mark 16:16; Acts 2:37–38). Believers who have had this required rebirth at the hands of those having authority have already been saved from sin *conditionally,* but they will not be saved *finally* until they have completed their mortal probation with the required continuing repentance, faithfulness, service, and enduring to the end.

Some Christians accuse Latter-day Saints who give this answer of denying the grace of God through claiming they can *earn* their salvation. We answer this accusation with the words of two Book of Mormon prophets. Nephi taught, "For we labor diligently . . . to persuade our children . . . to believe in Christ, and to be reconciled to God; for we know that it is by grace that we are saved, after all we can do" (2 Nephi 25:23). And what is "all we can do"? "All" surely includes repenting (Alma 24:11) and being baptized, keeping the commandments, and enduring to the end. Moroni pleaded, "Yea, come unto Christ, and be perfected in him, and deny yourselves of all ungodliness; and if ye shall deny yourselves of all ungodliness, and love God with all your might, mind and strength, then is his grace sufficient for you, that by his grace ye may be perfect in Christ" (Moroni 10:32).

We are not saved *in* our sins, as by being unconditionally saved through confessing Christ and then, inevitably, committing sins in our remaining lives (Alma 11:36–37). We are saved *from* our sins (Helaman 5:10) by a weekly renewal of our repentance and cleansing through the grace of God and his blessed plan of salvation (3 Nephi 9:20–22).

3. The question of whether a person has been saved is sometimes phrased in terms of whether that person has been "born again." Being "born again" is a familiar reference in the Bible and the Book of Mormon. As noted earlier, Jesus taught that except a man be "born again" (John 3:3), of water and of the Spirit, he cannot enter into the kingdom of God (John 3:5). The Book of Mormon has many teachings about the necessity of being "born again" or "born of God" (Mosiah 27:24–26; Alma 36:24, 26).

As we understand these scriptures, our answer to whether we have been born again is clearly, "Yes." We were born again when we entered into a covenant relationship with our Savior by being born of water and of the Spirit and by taking upon us the name of Jesus Christ. We can renew that rebirth each Sabbath when we partake of the sacrament.

Latter-day Saints affirm that those who have been born again in this way are spiritually begotten sons and daughters of Jesus Christ (Mosiah 5:7; 15:9–13; 27:25). Nevertheless, in order to realize the intended blessings of this born-again status, we must still keep our covenants and endure to the end. In the meantime, through the grace of God, we have been born again as new creatures with new spiritual parentage and the prospects of a glorious inheritance.

4. Another meaning of being saved is to be saved from the darkness of ignorance of God the Father and His Son, Jesus Christ, of the purpose of life, and of the destiny of men and women. The gospel made known to us by the teachings of Jesus

Christ has given us this salvation. "I am the light of the world," Jesus taught; "he that followeth me shall not walk in darkness, but shall have the light of life" (John 8:12; 12:46).

5. For Latter-day Saints, being "saved" can also mean being saved or delivered from the second death (meaning the final spiritual death) by assurance of a kingdom of glory in the world to come (1 Corinthians 15:40–42). Just as the Resurrection is universal, we affirm that every person who ever lived upon the face of the earth—except for a very few—is assured of salvation in this sense. As we read in modern revelation:

"And this is the gospel, the glad tidings . . . that he came into the world, even Jesus, to be crucified for the world, and to bear the sins of the world, and to sanctify the world, and to cleanse it from all unrighteousness;

"*That through him all might be saved* whom the Father had put into his power and made by him; who glorifies the Father, and *saves all the works of his hands,* except those sons of perdition who deny the Son after the Father has revealed him" (D&C 76:40–43; emphasis added).

President Brigham Young taught this doctrine when he declared that "every person who does not sin away the day of grace, and become an angel to the Devil, will be brought forth to inherit a kingdom of glory."[1] This meaning of *saved* ennobles the whole human race through the grace of our Lord and Savior, Jesus Christ. In this meaning of the word, all should answer, "Yes, I have been saved. Glory to God for the gospel and gift and grace of His Son!"

6. Finally, in another usage familiar and unique to Latter-day Saints, the words *saved* and *salvation* are also used to denote exaltation or eternal life (Abraham 2:11). This is sometimes referred to as the "fulness of salvation."[2] This salvation requires more than repentance and baptism by appropriate priesthood authority. It also requires the making of sacred covenants, including eternal marriage, in the temples of God, and faithfulness to those

covenants by enduring to the end. If we use the word *salvation* to mean exaltation, it is premature for any of us to say we have been "saved" in mortality. That glorious status can only follow the final judgment of Him who is the Great Judge of the living and the dead.

I have suggested that the short answer to the question of whether a faithful member of The Church of Jesus Christ of Latter-day Saints has been saved or born again must be a fervent, "Yes." Our covenant relationship with our Savior puts us in that "saved" or "born again" condition meant by those who ask this question. Some modern prophets have also used "salvation," or "saved," in this same present sense.

President Brigham Young declared, "It is present salvation and the present influence of the Holy Ghost that we need every day to keep us on saving ground. . . . I want present salvation. . . . Life is for us, and it is for us to receive it today, and not wait for the Millennium. Let us take a course to be saved today."[3] And President David O. McKay spoke of the revealed gospel of Jesus Christ in this same present sense of "salvation *here*—here and now."[4]

Members and leaders of The Church of Jesus Christ of Latter-day Saints face another important question: "Why do you send missionaries to preach to other Christians?" Sometimes this is asked with curiosity and sometimes with resentment.

My most memorable experience with that question occurred some years ago in what we then called the Eastern Bloc. After many years of Communist hostility to religion, these countries were suddenly and miraculously given a measure of religious freedom. When that door opened, many Christian faiths sent missionaries. As part of our preparation to do so, the First Presidency sent members of the Quorum of the Twelve Apostles to meet with government and church leaders in these countries. Our assignment was to introduce ourselves and explain what our missionaries would be doing.

Elder Russell M. Nelson and I called on the leader of the Orthodox Church in one of these countries. Here was a man who had helped keep the light of Christianity burning through the dark decades of Communist repression. I noted in my journal that he was a warm and gracious man who impressed me as a servant of the Lord. There was no spirit of arrogance or contention in our conversation of nearly an hour. Our visit was pleasant and cordial, filled with the goodwill that should always characterize conversations among men and women who love the Lord and seek to serve Him according to their own understandings.

Our host told us about the activities of his church during the period of Communist repression. He described the various difficulties his church and its work were experiencing as they emerged from that period and sought to regain their former position in the life of the country and in the hearts of the people. We introduced ourselves and our fundamental beliefs. We explained that we would soon be sending missionaries into his country and told him how they would perform their labors.

He asked, "Will your missionaries preach only to unbelievers, or will they also try to preach to believers?" We replied that our message was for everyone, believers as well as unbelievers. We gave two reasons for this answer—one a matter of principle and the other a matter of practicality. We told him that we preach to believers as well as unbelievers because our message, the restored gospel, makes an important addition to the knowledge, happiness, and peace of all mankind. As a matter of practicality, we preach to believers as well as unbelievers because we cannot tell the difference. I remember asking this distinguished leader, "When you stand before a congregation and look into the faces of the people, can you tell the difference between those who are real believers and those who are not?" He smiled wryly, and I sensed an admission that he had understood the point.

Through missionaries and members, the message of the restored gospel is going to all the world. To non-Christians, we witness of Christ and share the truths and ordinances of his restored gospel. To Christians we do the same. Even if a Christian has been "saved" in the familiar single sense discussed earlier, we teach that there remains more to be learned and more to be experienced. As President Gordon B. Hinckley has said, "[We are] not argumentative. We do not debate. We, in effect, simply say to others, 'Bring all the good that you have and let us see if we can add to it.'"[5]

The Church of Jesus Christ of Latter-day Saints offers all of the children of God the opportunity to learn the fulness of the gospel of Jesus Christ as restored in these latter days. We offer everyone the privilege of receiving all of the ordinances of salvation and exaltation. We invite all to hear this message, and we invite all who receive the confirming witness of the Spirit to heed it.

From an address published in the Ensign, *May 1998, 55–57.*

Notes

1. *Teachings of Presidents of the Church: Brigham Young,* Salt Lake City: The Church of Jesus Christ of Latter-day Saints, 1997, 288.
2. Bruce R. McConkie, *The Mortal Messiah,* 4 vols., Salt Lake City: Deseret Book, 1979–81, 1:242.
3. *Discourses of Brigham Young,* sel. John A. Widtsoe, Salt Lake City: Deseret Book, 1954, 15–16.
4. *Gospel Ideals,* comp. *The Improvement Era,* Salt Lake City: Deseret Book, 1953, 6.
5. "The BYU Experience," *Brigham Young University 1997–98 Speeches,* Provo, Utah: Brigham Young University Publications, 1998, 64.

13

SINS, CRIMES, AND ATONEMENT

AFTER ENOS CRIED TO THE LORD in mighty prayer all day and into the night, a voice came to him saying, "Enos, thy sins are forgiven thee, and thou shalt be blessed." Knowing that God could not lie, Enos understood that his guilt was swept away. Then he asked the question, "Lord, how is it done?" (Enos 1:5, 7).

It was done because of the Atonement and because of his faith in the Redeemer who paid the price (Enos 1:8). By an atonement that is both miraculous and beyond our comprehension, the vicarious sacrifice of the Lamb without blemish satisfies the *justice* of God. In this manner, we receive the *mercy* of God.

But what is *justice?* And what is *mercy?* And how do they relate to one another? These concepts are central to the gospel of Jesus Christ. They are sometimes misunderstood because they are easily confused with comparable concepts we understand from our mortal preoccupation with what we call the criminal law.

Indeed, our ideas about justice and mercy and the laws of God are sometimes shaped and confused by what we know about criminal justice as specified by the laws of man.

Some Latter-day Saints are susceptible to these misunderstandings. I have therefore chosen to discuss justice, mercy, and the Atonement, as well as repentance, confession, and suffering. I will compare and contrast how these realities relate to the content and enforcement of the laws of God and the laws of man.

Justice, Mercy, and the Atonement

Justice has many meanings. One is balance. A popular symbol of justice is scales in balance. Thus, when the laws of man have been violated, justice usually requires that a punishment be imposed, a penalty that will restore the balance.

People generally feel that justice has been done when an offender receives what he deserves—when the punishment fits the crime. The Church's declaration of belief states that "the commission of crime should be punished [under the laws of man] according to the nature of the offense" (D&C 134:8). The paramount concern of human law is justice.

Unlike the changeable laws of man, the laws of God are fixed and permanent, "irrevocably decreed in heaven before the foundations of this world" (D&C 130:20). These laws of God are likewise concerned with justice. The idea of justice as what one deserves is the fundamental premise of all scriptures that speak of men's being judged according to their works. Alma declared that it was "requisite with the justice of God that men should be judged according to their works" (Alma 41:3). The Savior told the Nephites that all men would stand before Him to be "judged of their works, whether they be good or whether they be evil" (3 Nephi 27:14). In his letter to the Romans, Paul described "the righteous judgment of God" in terms of "render[ing] to every man according to his deeds" (Romans 2:5–6).

According to eternal law, the consequences that follow from the justice of God are severe and permanent. When a commandment is broken, a commensurate penalty is imposed. This happens automatically. Punishments prescribed by the laws of man only follow the judge's action, but under the laws of God the consequences and penalties of sin are inherent in the act. "There is a law given, and a punishment affixed," the prophet Alma taught, and "justice claimeth the creature and executeth the law, and the law inflicteth the punishment." Alma explained, "And thus we see that all mankind were fallen, and they were in the grasp of justice; yea, the justice of God, which consigned them forever to be cut off from his presence" (Alma 42:22, 14). Abinadi added that the Lord "cannot deny justice when it has its claim" (Mosiah 15:27). By itself, justice is uncompromising.

The justice of God holds each of us responsible for our own transgressions and automatically imposes the penalty. This reality should permeate our understanding, and it should influence all our teachings about the commandments of God and the effect of individual transgressions.

In keeping with the legal traditions of man, many seem to want justice. It is true that justice is a friend that will protect us from persecution by the enemies of righteousness. But justice will also see that we receive what we deserve, and that is an outcome I fear. I cannot achieve my eternal goals on the basis of what I deserve. Though I try with all my might, I am still what King Benjamin called an "unprofitable servant" (Mosiah 2:21). To achieve my eternal goals, I need more than I deserve. I need more than justice.

This realization reminds me of an event that occurred in the law firm where I began practicing law more than forty years ago. A Chicago politician had been indicted for stuffing ballot boxes.

A partner in our firm told me how this politician came to his office to ask us to represent him in his criminal trial.

"What can you do for me?" he asked. Our partner replied that if this client retained our firm to conduct his defense, we would investigate the facts, research the law, and present the defense at the trial. "In this way," the lawyer concluded, "we will get you a fair trial."

The politician promptly stood up, put on his hat, and stalked out of the office. Pursuing him down the hall, the lawyer asked what he had said to offend him. "Nothing," the politician replied. "Then why are you leaving?" the lawyer asked. "The odds aren't good enough," the politician answered.

That man would not retain our firm to represent him in court because we would only promise him a fair trial, and he knew he needed more than that. He knew he was guilty, and he could only be saved from prison by something more favorable to him than justice.

Can justice save us? Can man in and of himself overcome the spiritual death all mankind suffers from the Fall, which we bring upon ourselves anew by our own sinful acts? No! Can we "work out our own salvation"? Never! "By the law no flesh is justified," Lehi explained (2 Nephi 2:5). "Salvation doth not come by the law alone," Abinadi warned (Mosiah 13:28). Shakespeare had one of his characters declare this truth: "In the course of justice, none of us should see salvation: we do pray for mercy."[1]

We know from numerous scriptures that "no unclean thing" can enter "the kingdom of God" (Moses 6:57; 1 Nephi 10:21; Alma 40:26). If we are to return to the presence of our Heavenly Father, we need the intervention of some powerful influence that transcends justice. That powerful intervention is the atonement of Jesus Christ.

The good news of the gospel is that because of the atonement of Jesus Christ there is something called *mercy. Mercy* signifies an advantage greater than what we deserve. This could come by the withholding of a deserved punishment or by the granting of an undeserved benefit.

If justice is balance, then mercy is counterbalance. If justice is exactly what we deserve, then mercy is *more* benefit than we deserve. In its relationship to justice and mercy, the Atonement is the means by which justice is served and mercy is extended. In combination, justice and mercy and the Atonement constitute the glorious eternal wholeness of the justice and mercy of God.

Mercy has several different manifestations in connection with our redemption. The universal resurrection from physical death is an unconditional act of mercy made possible by the Atonement. Alma taught Corianton that "mercy cometh because of the atonement; and the atonement bringeth to pass the resurrection of the dead" (Alma 42:23).

A second effect of the Atonement concerns our redemption from spiritual death. We are redeemed from the fall of Adam without condition. We are redeemed from the effects of our personal sins on condition of our obedience to the laws and ordinances of the gospel.

Justice is served and mercy is extended by the suffering and shed blood of Jesus Christ. The Messiah "offereth himself a sacrifice for sin, to answer the ends of the law" (2 Nephi 2:7; Romans 5:18–19). In this way, "God himself atoneth for the sins of the world, to bring about the plan of mercy, to appease the demands of justice, that God might be a perfect, just God, and a merciful God also" (Alma 42:15).

We are all dependent upon the mercy God the Father extended to all mankind through the atoning sacrifice of our Lord and Savior, Jesus Christ. This is the central reality of the gospel. This is why we "talk of Christ, we rejoice in Christ, we preach of Christ . . . that our children may know to what source they may look for a remission of their sins" (2 Nephi 25:26).

The reality of our total dependence upon Jesus Christ for the attainment of our goals of immortality and eternal life should dominate every teaching and every testimony and every action of every soul touched by the light of the restored gospel. If we teach every other subject and principle with perfection and fall short on this one, we have failed in our most important mission.

Laws of Man and Laws of God

Now let us compare and contrast the laws of God and the laws of man. The laws of God achieve their purposes through justice, mercy, and the atonement of Jesus Christ. In contrast, the laws of man focus on justice; they have no theory of mercy, and they take no account of the Atonement. This contrast fosters the confusion I mentioned at the outset.

I will now proceed to consider the similar and contrasting positions of the laws of man and the laws of God on some related subjects, such as repentance, confession, and suffering.

The Requirement of Repentance

1. *Necessity.* The benefits of the Atonement are subject to the conditions prescribed by Him who paid the price. The conditions include repentance. The requirement of repentance is one of the principal contrasts between the laws of God and the laws of man.

God has told us through His prophets that only those who repent are forgiven (D&C 1:32; 58:42). Elder Bruce R. McConkie said it tersely: The Messiah brought "mercy to the repentant and justice to the unrepentant."[2] Alma taught that "the plan of redemption could not be brought about, only on conditions of repentance of men in this probationary state" (Alma 42:13). Amulek said that "he that exercises no faith unto repentance is exposed to the whole law of the demands of justice" (Alma 34:16). Finally, in this dispensation our Redeemer declared, "If they would not repent they must suffer even as I" (D&C 19:17).

These eternal truths, fundamental in the doctrine of the

restored gospel, explain why our church discipline is concerned with assisting a transgressor to repent. These truths also explain why evidence of repentance is the most important single factor in determining what church discipline is necessary to accomplish its principal purpose—to save the soul of the transgressor.

The redemptive function of church discipline and the revelation necessary for its implementation have no counterpart in the laws of man.

2. *Confession.* A second contrast concerns the role of the criminal's or the transgressor's confession. Under the laws of man, a confession only serves the function of strong evidence of guilt. It is not essential because an accused person can be found guilty without a confession if the other evidence of guilt is sufficient.

Under the laws of God, a confession is absolutely essential because there is no repentance without confession. An early apostle taught, "If we confess our sins, he is faithful and just to forgive us our sins, and to cleanse us from all unrighteousness" (John 1:9). And in modern revelation the Lord declared, "By this ye may know if a man repenteth of his sins—behold, he will confess them and forsake them" (D&C 58:43; 61:2; 64:7).

Repentance begins when we recognize that we have done wrong. We might call this "confession to self." This occurs, President Spencer W. Kimball said, when a person is willing "to convict himself of the transgression without soft-pedaling or minimizing the error, to be willing to face facts, meet the issue, and pay necessary penalties—and until the person is in this frame of mind he has not begun to repent."[3]

The next step, for all our sins, is to confess them to the Lord in prayer. In addition, when the sins are of a serious nature, they must be confessed to the priesthood leader designated by the Lord—the bishop, branch president, or stake president. Elder Marion G. Romney described the sins that must be confessed to the bishop as those transgressions "of such a nature as would, unrepented of, put in jeopardy his right to membership or fellowship in the Church of Jesus Christ."⁴ These last two confessions are what the Lord prescribed when He referred to "confessing thy sins unto thy brethren, and before the Lord" (D&C 59:12).

3. *Restitution.* A third contrast concerns restitution. Restitution is also an essential ingredient of repentance. Transgressors must do all they can to restore what their transgression has taken from others. This includes confession to and seeking the forgiveness of those they have wronged. It also includes making the disclosures necessary to protect those who have been put in jeopardy by their wrongdoing. For example, they may need to alert other persons to health or safety hazards the wrongdoer's actions have created. As part of restitution, transgressors may also need to make disclosures to civil authorities and to accept the consequences.

Transgressors should look on the necessity for restitution— restoring what they have taken from others—as a privilege. When restitution can be made, repentance is easier. When the transgression is such that restitution is very difficult or even impossible, then repentance is also very difficult or even impossible. For example, the most serious sins include murder, adultery, and fornication. It is no coincidence that these are transgressions for which restitution is difficult or impossible. What this comparison means is that if something is wrong and it cannot be undone, never, never, never do it. I wish every young man or woman would understand and practice that simple and vital principle. This does not mean that we are free to do wrong things that can be repaired by restitution, like stealing. They are sins too. The point is that it is probably easier to repent of stealing, after which you *can* make restitution, than it is to repent of something like sexual abuse, after which you cannot make restitution.

Restitution has far less significance under the laws of man. While criminal courts will sometimes sentence a defendant to restore what he took from a victim, such restitution is, at best, an incidental concern of the punishment meted out by the judge of a criminal court.

4. *Suffering.* The fourth contrast, suffering, is probably the most misunderstood ingredient of repentance. This misunderstanding may result from the fact that there is a great gulf between the simple role of suffering under the laws of man and its very complex role under the laws of God.

The laws of man deliberately inflict punishment to make a criminal suffer for his crime. Punishment is a principal object of the laws of man. Criminal courts seek to make an offender "pay" for his wrongdoing, and this is done without regard to whether the offender is repentant or unrepentant.

Some have looked on church discipline in the same light. But the suggestion that a Church officer or a disciplinary council is supposed to punish a transgressor or make him suffer to pay for his wrongdoing misunderstands the purpose of church discipline and its relationship (and the relationship of suffering) to repentance, mercy, and the Atonement.

Unrepentant Transgressors

Under the law and justice of God, sinners are punished. Through the prophet Isaiah, the Lord said He would "punish the inhabitants of the earth for their iniquity" (Isaiah 26:21). Alma taught that God's law could not exist "save there was a punishment," and that there is "a punishment affixed" for every sin (Alma 42:17–18; Amos 3:1–2). Our second article of faith states our basic belief that men will be punished for their own sins.

Justice requires that the *unrepentant* transgressor suffer for his own sins. Perhaps the greatest statement of this principle in all the scriptures is the revelation the Lord gave to the Prophet Joseph Smith in March 1830, the month the Book of Mormon was published and the month before the Church was organized (D&C 19). There the Lord reminded us of "the great day of judgment" when all will be judged according to their works. He explained that the "endless" or "eternal" punishment that comes from sin is not punishment without end; rather, it is the punishment of God, who is endless and eternal (D&C 19: 3, 6, 10–12).

In this setting, the Savior of the world commanded us to repent and keep His commandments. "Repent, lest . . . your sufferings be sore—how sore you know not, how exquisite you know not, yea, how hard to bear you know not. For behold, I, God, have suffered these things for all, that they might not suffer if they would repent; but if they would not repent they must suffer even as I" (D&C 19:15–17).

Repentant Transgressors

What about repentant transgressors? Are they punished? Must they suffer? The punishment that leads to repentance and the punishment that makes repentance possible must include suffering, but whose suffering is this—the sinner's or the Savior's?

Let us recall two scriptures: (1) Alma's statement that "repentance could not come unto men except there were a punishment" (Alma 42:16) and (2) the Savior's revelation that He had "suffered these things for all, that they might not suffer if they would repent; but if they would not repent they must suffer even as I" (D&C 19:16–17).

Do these scriptures mean that a person who repents does not need to suffer at all because the entire punishment is borne by the Savior? That cannot be the meaning because it would be inconsistent with the Savior's other teachings.

What is meant is that the person who repents does not need to suffer "even as" the Savior suffered for that sin. Sinners who are repenting will experience some suffering, but, because of their repentance and because of the Atonement, they will not experience the full "exquisite" extent of eternal torment the Savior suffered for that sin.

President Spencer W. Kimball, who gave such comprehensive teachings on repentance and forgiveness, said that personal suffering "is a very important part of repentance. One has not begun to repent until he has suffered intensely for his sins. . . . If a person hasn't suffered, he hasn't repented. . . . He has got to go through a change in his system whereby he suffers and then forgiveness is a possibility."[5]

Lehi taught this principle when he said that the Savior's atoning sacrifice was for "all those who have a broken heart and a contrite spirit; and unto none else can the ends of the law be answered" (2 Nephi 2:7). The repentant sinner who comes to Christ with a broken heart and a contrite spirit has been through a process of personal pain and suffering for sin. He understands the meaning of Alma's statement that "none but the truly penitent are saved" (Alma 42:24).

Elder Bruce C. Hafen has described how some people think that repentance is too easy. He said they look "for shortcuts and easy answers, thinking that quick confessions or breezy apologies alone are enough."[6] President Kimball said, "Very frequently people think they have repented and are worthy of forgiveness when all they have done is to express sorrow or regret at the unfortunate happening."[7]

There is a big difference between the "godly sorrow [that] worketh repentance" (2 Corinthians 7:10), which involves personal suffering, and the easy and relatively painless sorrow for being caught, or the misplaced sorrow Mormon described as "the sorrowing of the damned, because the Lord would not always suffer them to take happiness in sin" (Mormon 2:13).

Alma the Younger certainly understood that easy and painless sorrow was not a sufficient basis for repentance. His experience, related in detail in the Book of Mormon, is our best scriptural illustration of the fact that the process of repentance is filled with personal suffering for sin. Alma said that after he was stopped in his wicked course, he was "in the darkest abyss" (Mosiah 27:29), "racked with eternal torment, for my soul was harrowed up to the greatest degree and racked with all my sins. Yea, I did remember all my sins and iniquities, for which I was tormented with the pains of hell" (Alma 36:12–13).

He told how "the very thought of coming into the presence of my God did rack my soul with inexpressible horror." He spoke of being "harrowed up by the memory of [his] many sins." After three days and three nights of what he called "the most bitter pain and anguish of soul," he cried out to the Lord Jesus Christ for mercy, and he received "a remission of [his] sins" (Alma 36:14, 17; 38:8).

All of our experience confirms the fact that we must endure personal suffering in the process of repentance—and for serious transgressions that suffering can be severe and prolonged. I believe that every one of us who is truly honest with himself or herself recognizes the truth of this principle. We have felt it in our own lives, and we have seen it in the lives of others.

We should also observe that our personal suffering for sin is private, not public. Often only the sinner and the Lord and the Lord's servant know what is happening. In contrast to the public nature of the punishment inflicted by the laws of man, the suffering that leads to mercy under the laws of God is intensely personal.

The Savior

What about the suffering of the Savior? The laws of man obviously take no account of this. Under the laws of God, the Savior's suffering for sin is of supreme importance. The suffering that impels a transgressor toward repentance is personal suffering. But the suffering that satisfies the demands of justice for all repented transgressions is the suffering of our Savior and Redeemer. He suffered for the sins of all, "that they might not suffer if they would repent" (D&C 19:16). In the great words of Isaiah, "He was wounded for our transgressions, he was bruised for our iniquities: the chastisement of our peace was upon him;

and with his stripes we are healed" (Isaiah 53:5). If we will only repent, the Redeemer's suffering has paid the price for our sins.

The Savior's suffering is vastly different from every other suffering for sin. The suffering of the sinner is the suffering of the guilty. The suffering of the Savior was the suffering of the pure and sinless. His suffering was entirely undeserved. He was "wounded for our transgressions," not His own. As the prophet Amulek explained, "there can be nothing which is short of an infinite atonement which will suffice for the sins of the world" (Alma 34:12). And, as the Apostle Peter said, the blood that was shed and the sacrifice that was made to redeem us had to be "the precious blood of Christ, as of a lamb without blemish and without spot" (1 Peter 1:19).

To summarize, the Atonement has no counterpart in the laws of man, and the laws of man take no account of the various elements of repentance and the different kinds of suffering that are accounted under the laws of God.

In contrast to the punishment that is the intended result of the judgment of a criminal court, the primary purpose of church discipline is to facilitate repentance—to qualify a transgressor for the mercy of God and the salvation made possible through the atonement of Jesus Christ. Personal suffering is inevitably part of that process, but personal suffering is not its purpose.

Church discipline is not an instrument of punishment but a catalyst for change. The purpose of the personal suffering that must occur as part of the process of repentance is not to punish the transgressor but to change him. The broken heart and contrite spirit required to "answer the ends of the law" (2 Nephi 2:7) introduce the repentant transgressor to the change necessary to conform his life to the pattern prescribed by his Redeemer. The major concern of the laws of God is to perfect the lives of God's children.

Like wayward Corianton, some transgressors have difficulty understanding "the justice of God in the punishment of the sinner" (Alma 42:1). And they do not understand the conditions of mercy. "Why must I suffer at all?" they ask. "Now that I have said I am sorry, why can't you just give me mercy and forget about this?" Such questions have some force under the laws of man. Under those laws, mercy can rob justice (as happens in the case of a pardon or executive clemency).

In contrast, under the laws of God mercy cannot rob justice. The sinner must repent or pay the full penalty of suffering for his sins. The object of God's laws is to save the sinner, not simply to punish him. Consequently, there is no exemption from the conditions a transgressor must meet to qualify for the mercy necessary for salvation. The repentant transgressor must be changed, and the conditions of repentance, including confession and personal suffering, are essential to accomplish that change. To exempt a transgressor from those conditions would deprive him of the change necessary for his salvation. That would be neither just nor merciful.

Change of Life

The final contrast between the laws of God and the laws of man concerns their different level of concern with a change of life.

We tend to think of the results of repentance as simply cleansing us from sin. That is an incomplete view of the matter. A person who sins is like a tree that bends easily in the wind. On a windy and rainy day the tree may bend so deeply against the ground that the leaves become soiled with mud, like sin. If we only focus on cleaning the leaves, the weakness in the tree that allowed it to bend and soil its leaves may remain. Merely cleansing the leaves does not strengthen the tree. Similarly, a person who is merely sorry to be soiled by sin will sin again in the next high wind. The susceptibility to repetition will continue until the tree has been strengthened.

When we have gone through the process that results in what the scriptures call a broken heart and a contrite spirit, the Savior does more than cleanse us from sin. He also gives us new strength. The new strength we receive from the Savior is essential for us to realize the purpose of our cleansing from sin, which is to return to our Heavenly Father. To be admitted to His presence, we must be more than clean. We must also be changed from a morally weak person who has transgressed into a strong person with the spiritual stature to dwell in the presence of God. We must, as the scripture says, become "a saint through the atonement of Christ the Lord" (Mosiah 3:19). This is what the scripture means in its explanation that a person who has repented of sins will forsake them (D&C 58:43). Forsaking sins is more than resolving not to repeat them. Forsaking involves a fundamental change in the individual.

King Benjamin and Alma both spoke of "a mighty change of heart." King Benjamin's congregation described that mighty change by saying that they had "no more disposition to do evil, but to do good continually" (Mosiah 5:2). Alma illustrated that change of heart when he described a people who "awoke unto God," "put their trust in [him]," and were "faithful until the end." He challenged others to "look forward with an eye of faith" to the time when we will "stand before God to be judged" according to our deeds (Alma 5: 7, 13, 15). Persons who have had that change in their hearts have attained the strength and stature to dwell with God. That is what we call being saved.

Avoid Sin

Some Latter-day Saints who wrongly think repentance is easy maintain that a little sinning will not hurt. Young people of this persuasion may say, "It is okay to have a few free ones because it is easy to repent before your mission or marriage." The adult versions are more sophisticated and more pernicious. Perhaps some would even assert that a person is better off after he has sinned and repented. "Get a little experience with sin," one argument goes, "and then you will be better able to counsel and sympathize with sinners. You can always repent."

I plead with my brothers and sisters, my young friends and my older friends, avoid transgression! The idea that one can deliberately sin and easily repent or that one is better off after sinning and repenting are devilish lies of the adversary. Would anyone seriously contend that it is better to learn firsthand that a certain blow will break a bone or that a certain mixture of chemicals will explode and burn off our skin? Are we better off after we have sustained and then scarred over from such injuries? It is obviously better to heed the warnings of wise persons who know the effects of certain traumas on our bodies.

Just as we can benefit from someone else's experience in matters such as these, we can also benefit from the warnings contained in the commandments of God. We do not have to have personal experience with the effects of serious transgressions to know that they are injurious to our souls and destructive of our eternal welfare.

Some years ago one of our sons asked me why it was not a good idea to try alcohol and tobacco to see what they were like. He knew about the Word of Wisdom, and he also knew the health effects of these substances, but he was questioning why he should not just try them out for himself. I replied that if he wanted to try something out he ought to go to a barnyard and eat a little manure. He recoiled in horror. "Ooh, that's gross," he reacted.

"I'm glad you think so," I said, "but why don't you just try it out so you will know for yourself? While you are proposing to try one thing that you know is not good for you, why don't you apply that principle to some others?" That illustration of the silliness of "trying it out for yourself" proved persuasive to one sixteen-year-old.

Hope Versus Discouragement

Many among the young think that repentance is easy. At the opposite extreme are those who think that repentance is hard.

Our youth include many of these also. This group of souls is so tenderhearted and conscientious that its members see sin everywhere in their own lives, and they despair of ever being able to be clean. A call for repentance that is clear enough and loud enough to encourage reformation by the lenient can produce paralyzing discouragement in the conscientious. The dose of doctrine that is strong enough to penetrate the hard shell of the easygoing group may prove to be a massive overdose for the conscientious. This is a common problem. We are never free from the reality that a doctrinal overdose for some is a doctrinal "underdose" for others.

We must make a special effort to counteract the discouragement and despair that Satan uses so skillfully to overpower the struggling. President Ezra Taft Benson gave inspired counsel on this subject. Writing in the *Ensign* in the first year of his presidency, he said:

"We live in an age when, as the Lord foretold, men's hearts are failing them, not only physically but in spirit. (See D&C 45:26.) Many are giving up heart for the battle of life. Suicide ranks as a major cause of deaths of college students. As the showdown between good and evil approaches with its accompanying trials and tribulations, Satan is increasingly striving to overcome the Saints with despair, discouragement, despondency, and depression.

"Yet, of all people, we as Latter-day Saints should be the most optimistic and the least pessimistic. For while we know that 'peace shall be taken from the earth, and the devil shall have power over his own dominion,' we are also assured that 'the Lord shall have power over his saints, and shall reign in their midst.' (D&C 1:35–36.)"[8]

President Benson then reviewed a dozen ways we can combat despondency, including repentance, prayer, service, priesthood blessings, wholesome music, and just plain endurance. On that last suggestion he gave this memorable advice: "There are times when you simply have to righteously hang on and outlast the devil until his depressive spirit leaves you."[9]

One of Satan's most potent techniques of discouragement is to deny the power of the Atonement by persuading a sinner that God cannot or will not forgive. Or, Satan may seek to persuade a sinner that he is so depraved that he must not forgive himself. We should teach the discouraged that part of the process of repentance is to let go of our sins, to yield them up to God and follow His example by forgiving ourselves as He forgave us.

In conclusion, President Benson said: "We can rise above the enemies of despair, depression, discouragement, and despondency by remembering that God provides righteous alternatives, some of which I have mentioned. As it states in the Bible, 'There hath no temptation taken you but such as is common to man: but God is faithful, who will not suffer you to be tempted above that ye are able; but will with the temptation also make a way to escape, that ye may be able to bear it' (1 Corinthians 10:13)."[10]

The love of God is manifest in the Atonement, and we accept that love when we practice the principle of repentance. Repentance is a continuing process, needed by all because "all have sinned, and come short of the glory of God" (Romans 3:23). Full repentance is possible, and forgiveness is certain.

How precious the promise that God will take "away the guilt from our hearts, through the merits of his Son" (Alma 24:10). How comforting the promise that "though your sins be as scarlet, they shall be as white as snow" (Isaiah 1:18). How glorious God's own promise that "he who has repented of his sins, the same is forgiven, and I, the Lord, remember them no more" (D&C 58:42; Jeremiah 31:34; Hebrews 8:12).

By His atoning sacrifice, our Savior brought about what Amulek called "the bowels of mercy, which overpowereth justice" (Alma 34:15). The relationship between justice and mercy and the Atonement is nowhere more succinctly or beautifully expressed than by Eliza R. Snow in the fifth verse of that wonderful hymn "How Great the Wisdom and the Love":

How great, how glorious, how complete,
Redemption's grand design,
Where justice, love, and mercy meet
In harmony divine![11]

And so we join our voices with the prophet Jacob, who declared that "my soul delighteth in the covenants of the Lord . . . in his grace, and in his justice, and power, and mercy in the great and eternal plan of deliverance from death" (2 Nephi 11:5).

From an address delivered to Church Education System educators on February 7, 1992; for further discussion pertaining to Church discipline, see the author's The Lord's Way, *209–50.*

NOTES

1. *The Merchant of Venice,* act 4, scene 1, lines 196–197.
2. *The Promised Messiah,* Salt Lake City: Deseret Book, 1978, 337.
3. *Teachings of Spencer W. Kimball,* ed. Edward L. Kimball, Salt Lake City: Bookcraft, 1982, 86.
4. In Conference Report, October 1955, 125.
5. *Teachings of Spencer W. Kimball,* 88, 99.
6. *The Broken Heart,* Salt Lake City: Deseret Book, 1989, 150.
7. *Teachings of Spencer W. Kimball,* 87.
8. "Do Not Despair," *Ensign,* October 1986, 2.
9. "Do Not Despair," 5.
10. "Do Not Despair," 5.
11. *Hymns of The Church of Jesus Christ of Latter-day Saints,* Salt Lake City: The Church of Jesus Christ of Latter-day Saints, 1985, no. 195.

14

SINS AND MISTAKES

THE IDEA THAT EDUCATION SHOULD be based on both reason and revelation is a true gospel principle. It is rooted in the divine direction that we "seek learning, even by study and also by faith" (D&C 88:118). It is an immensely important principle that some good persons do not understand and apply. Some who have refined their application of reason reject revelation, and some who understand revelation seem to misunderstand its relationship with reason.

We can be edified by the example of great Latter-day Saints who honor and apply both reason and revelation. Arthur Henry King, a distinguished British civil servant who became a professor at Brigham Young University and then president of the London Temple, was such an individual. I quote from his book, *The Abundance of the Heart:*

"Conversion is not a matter of choosing what we like and

ignoring the rest, but of whole-minded acceptance. . . . When we have performed this act of faith, . . . all the difficulties are resolved by it. When we have laid down at Christ's feet all our scholarship, all our learning, all the tools of our trades, we discover that we may pick them all up again, clean them, adjust them, and use them for the Church in the name of Christ and in the light of his countenance. We do not need to discard them. All we need to do is to use them from the faith which now possesses us. And we find that we can."[1]

Those words are both a challenge for all of us and an appropriate introduction for what I wish to discuss. I wish to reason about a basic principle given in modern revelation but not as well understood or applied as it should be. This principle was given to guide us in our relationships with one another. It is especially important for parents with teenage children.

Three verses of the Doctrine and Covenants identify an important contrast between sins and mistakes. I had never seen these verses until I read the Doctrine and Covenants for the fifteenth or twentieth time. Their direction came to my mind with such freshness and impact that I thought they might have been newly inserted in my book. That is the way with prayerful study of the scriptures. The scriptures do not change, but we do, and so the old scriptures can give us new insights every time we read them.

The twentieth section of the Doctrine and Covenants, given the same month the Church was organized, is the basic revelation on Church government. It contains one verse giving this important direction: "Any member of the church of Christ transgressing, or being overtaken in a fault, shall be dealt with as the scriptures direct" (D&C 20:80).

The clear implication of this verse is that "transgressing" is different from being "overtaken in a fault," but that either type of action is to be dealt with as the scriptures direct.

The scriptures contain various directions for dealing with

members, but the key direction for present purposes is contained in two verses in the November 1831 revelation given as the preface to the book that is now the Doctrine and Covenants. These verses follow the Lord's explanation that He has given His servants the commandments in the Doctrine and Covenants "after the manner of their language, that they might come to understanding" (D&C 1:24). Succeeding verses clarify the difference between error and sin, and give distinctly different directions for the correction of each.

"And inasmuch as they erred it might be made known. And inasmuch as they sinned they might be chastened, that they might repent" (D&C 1:25, 27).

Under these verses, "transgressing" is different from being at "fault," and to err is different than to sin. Here I need to define some terms. I believe that in these scriptures and for purposes of the subject of this chapter, "sin" and "transgression" mean the same thing. Similarly, to "err" or to be at "fault" are also equivalent. In referring to this second category I will use the more familiar description, "to make a mistake."

My subject is the contrast between sins and mistakes. Both can hurt us and both require attention, but the scriptures direct a different treatment. Chewing on a live electrical cord or diving headfirst into water of uncertain depth are mistakes that should be made known so that they can be corrected. Violations of the commandments of God are sins that require chastening and repentance. In the treatment process we should not require repentance for mistakes, but we are commanded to preach the necessity of repentance for sins. That is my message.

My first illustration of this principle uses words I learned as a young boy reading the Sears Roebuck catalog. In those days, Sears offered each item of merchandise in the catalog in three different qualities: good, better, and best. Sears did not use the word *bad,* but if I could add that word I would have four words that permit me to illustrate my first point with clarity. For most of us, most of the time, the choice between good and bad is easy. What usually causes us difficulty is determining which uses of our time and influence are merely good, or better, or best. Applying that fact to the question of sins and mistakes, I would say that a wrong choice in the contest between what is good and what is bad is a sin, but a poor choice among things that are good, better, and best is merely a mistake.

Mortals make those kinds of mistakes all the time. We can read some of them in Church history. I believe some of the persecutions our Latter-day Saint forefathers endured were a result of their sins. The Lord told them so by revelation (D&C 101:2). I believe some of their persecutions were also the result of mistakes. Thus, Sidney Rigdon's inflammatory "salt sermon," which contributed to conditions that brought about the Saints' expulsion from Missouri, was probably a mistake. Similarly, some mistaken decisions on Kirtland banking policies plagued the Saints for more than a decade. These financial difficulties were perhaps portended in the Lord's warning to the Prophet Joseph Smith, "And in temporal labors thou shalt not have strength, for this is not thy calling" (D&C 24:9).

On a more personal level, consider the mistake described by Truman G. Madsen in his fine book, *Joseph Smith the Prophet*. In a relaxed moment one day the Prophet turned to his secretary, Howard Coray, and said, "Brother Coray I wish you were a little larger. I would like to have some fun with you," meaning wrestling. Brother Coray said, "Perhaps you can as it is." The Prophet reached and grappled him and twisted him over—and broke his leg. All compassion, he carried him home, put him in bed, and splinted and bandaged his leg.[2]

In teaching the Saints not to accuse one another, the prophet Joseph Smith said, "What many people call sin is not sin."[3] I believe the large category of actions that are mistakes rather than sins illustrates the truth of that statement. If we would be more understanding of one another's mistakes, being satisfied merely to correct and not to chasten or call to repentance, we would surely promote loving and living together in greater peace and harmony.

The appropriateness of that approach as applied to mistakes is surely illustrated by the Prophet Joseph Smith's well-known teachings to the first Relief Society. He taught the sisters to be kind and loving toward those who made mistakes, and also toward sinners. He said:

"Suppose that Jesus Christ and holy angels should object to us on frivolous things, what would become of us? We must be merciful to one another, and overlook small things. . . .

"Nothing is so much calculated to lead people to forsake sin as to take them by the hand, and watch over them with tenderness. When persons manifest the least kindness and love to me, O what power it has over my mind, while the opposite course has a tendency to harrow up all the harsh feelings and depress the human mind. . . . There should be no license for sin, but mercy should go hand in hand with reproof."[4]

The book of Proverbs is filled with advice on mistakes or errors, and the word most frequently applied to the person who fails to behave appropriately in these areas is *fool.* Our dictionary defines a fool as a person lacking in judgment or prudence. A fool is a fool, not a sinner. Our English writers understood that difference and used it in their frequent contrast of fools and knaves.

Proverbs says, "A fool uttereth all his mind: but a wise man keepeth it in till afterwards" (Proverbs 29:11). The Old Testament's usage of the word fool is evident in Saul's confession: "I have played the fool, and have erred exceedingly" (1 Samuel 26:21). Stimulated by that expression, a playwright penned these lines, which remind us of mortality's abundant field for foolish conduct.

> When we play the fool, how wide
> The theater expands! beside,
> How long the audience sits before us!
> How many prompters! what a chorus![5]

The Savior used the term fool to characterize the lesson in

His parable about the rich man who built greater barns to store his abundant fruits and goods, and then said to his soul, "Thou hast much goods laid up for many years; take thine ease, eat, drink, and be merry" (Luke 12:19). Then, the Savior taught, "God said unto him, Thou fool, this night thy soul shall be required of thee: then whose shall those things be, which thou hast provided? So is he that layeth up treasure for himself, and is not rich toward God" (Luke 12:20–21).

The distinction between sins and mistakes is important to our actions in the realm of politics and public policy debates. We have seen some very bitter finger-pointing among Latter-day Saints who disagree with one another on the policies our government should follow, the political parties we should support, or the persons we should elect as our public servants. Such disagreements are inevitable in representative government. But it is not inevitable that disagreements result in the personal denunciations and bitter feelings described in the press or encountered in personal conversations.

When we understand the difference between sins and mistakes, we realize that almost all our disagreements in elections and public policy debates are matters of error (mistake) rather than transgression (sin). The inspired direction for such differences of opinion is to try to correct the errors by pointing them out in civil discourse but not to chasten or denounce as sinners those we think have committed them. (Of course, some public policies are so intertwined with moral issues that there may be only one morally right position, but that is rare).

In an interview with the press, President Howard W. Hunter said that one of our objectives as a church is "to change the world and its thinking." Identifying how we need to go about that task, President Hunter said, "We have an obligation, as Christians—as members of the Church—and we call upon all people to be more kind and more considerate—whether it be in our homes, in our businesses, in our relations in society." Concluding this plea, he said that we have a responsibility to teach "a Christ-like response to all the problems of the world."[6] Understanding and applying the distinction between sins and mistakes will help us fulfill that divinely imposed responsibility.

The scriptures and our leaders have also taught us principles that require a loving approach to those with whom we have any kind of disagreement on matters of religious belief. In one of the great prophecies that concluded his ministry, the prophet Nephi described the false churches of the last days that would teach "false and vain and foolish doctrines" (2 Nephi 28:9). He denounced many of their followers for obvious wickedness, including robbing the poor and committing whoredoms. Then, he referred to another group, an exceptional few who were the humble followers of Christ. Note the words he used to describe these two groups:

"They have all gone astray save it be a few, who are the humble followers of Christ; nevertheless, they are led, that in many instances they do err because they are taught by the precepts of men" (2 Nephi 28:14).

Here we see that when humble followers of Christ are led astray by the precepts of men their offense is error, not transgression.

Elder George A. Smith applied that principle in an address delivered in the Tabernacle in Salt Lake City in 1870. Referring to honest persons in the Christian world at the time of the Restoration who had been led astray as to doctrine, he used the word error and indicated that the Lord would be merciful to them.

"There were, however, honest persons in all of the denominations, and God has respect to every man who is honest of heart and purpose, though he may be deceived, and in error as to principle and doctrine; yet so far as that error is the result of their being deceived by the cunning craftiness of men, or of circumstances over which such have no control, the Lord in His abundant mercy looks with allowance thereon, and in His great economy He has provided different glories and ordained that all persons shall be judged according to the knowledge they possess and the use they make of that knowledge, and according to the deeds done in the body, whether good or evil."[7]

Elder Smith's explanation obviously relied on the doctrine that defines the degree of responsibility of persons who have not received the law. The Apostle Paul taught that we sin only when we know the law (Romans 7:7). In a clear elaboration of that principle, the prophet Jacob affirms that "where there is no law given . . . there is no condemnation" (2 Nephi 9:25). As a result, he taught that "the atonement satisfieth the demands of his justice upon all those who have not the law given to them" (2 Nephi 9:26; Alma 42:17). Similarly, the prophet Mormon declared "that all little children are alive in Christ, and also all they that are without the law. For the power of redemption cometh on all them that have no law" (Moroni 8:22).

This is the principle another Book of Mormon prophet applied in teaching the wicked Nephites that unless they would repent, it would be better for the Lamanites than for them. "For behold, they are more righteous than you, for they have not sinned against that great knowledge which ye have received; therefore the Lord will be merciful unto them; . . . even when thou shalt be utterly destroyed except thou shalt repent" (Helaman 7:24).

Under this doctrine, persons who break a law that has not been given to them are not accountable for sins. Of course, all men have been given the Spirit of Christ (conscience) that they may "know good from evil" (2 Nephi 2:5; Moroni 7:16). This makes us all aware of the wrongfulness of certain conduct, such as taking a life or stealing, but it does not make men accountable for laws that need to be specifically taught, like the knowledge that had been received by the Nephites but not the Lamanites (Helaman 7:24). Persons who break those kinds of laws when they have not received them are guilty of mistakes that should be corrected, but they are not accountable for sins. They may suffer for their mistakes, like a smoker suffers for breaking a law of health even if he has never heard of the Word of Wisdom. Errors and mistakes may have inherent penalties, but their perpetrators should not be branded as sinners.

We understand from our doctrine that before the age of accountability a child is "not capable of committing sin" (Moroni 8:8). During that time, children can commit mistakes, even very serious and damaging ones that must be corrected, but their acts are not accountable as sins.

Even after children reach the age of accountability, before we parents chasten them as sinners for wrongful actions, we should ask ourselves whether we have taught them the wrongfulness of that conduct. Have we taught them the commandments of God on that matter? This is a profound challenge and lesson for parents. Perhaps this is the underlying principle for the Lord's solemn declaration that "inasmuch as parents have children in Zion, or in any of her stakes which are organized, that teach them not to understand the doctrine of repentance, faith in Christ the Son of the living God, and of baptism and the gift of the Holy Ghost by the laying on of the hands, when eight years old, the sin be upon the heads of the parents" (D&C 68:25).

The application of the commandments is sometimes difficult for children to understand. As parents we know that we must be constantly teaching our children how to apply the commandments to the varying circumstances of their lives. For example, without explicit teaching they may not understand that stealing services from a long-distance company is just as much a violation of the eighth commandment as stealing inventory from a retail merchant. In some of these teaching efforts, on matters that are genuinely in doubt, parents may need to treat an uninformed or untaught act as the equivalent of a mistake rather than a sin. We should correct the youthful offenders and promptly teach them correct principles to guide their future actions. Any repetition would then be a transgression.

This redemptive procedure also applies in the definition of the adult transgression of apostasy for teaching false doctrine. Knowing that there may be genuine questions about what is false doctrine, the servants of the Lord have specified a procedure for protecting a member who strays over the line innocently. This kind of apostasy is defined as persisting "in teaching as Church doctrine information that is not Church doctrine after [being] corrected by their bishops or higher authority."[8] In other words, the teaching of false doctrine may be classified as a mistake the first time it happens, but it becomes a sin and a subject for Church discipline after those in authority clarify the application of the law to what the member is teaching.

Even though they have taught their children all the commandments and principles they need for righteous and provident living, parents are still susceptible to the serious error of failing to distinguish between mistakes and sins. If well-meaning parents call teenagers to repentance for teenagers' numerous mistakes, they may dilute the effect of chastisement and reduce the impact of repentance for the category of teenage sins that really requires it. This point is well illustrated in an experience shared in an interview on Richard and Linda Eyre's television series "Families are Forever."

The subject was the importance of being friends with our teenage children and creating an atmosphere in which they are free to communicate with us. In illustrating that important point, LDS filmmaker Kieth Merrill gave an equally valuable illustration of the importance of distinguishing between errors and transgressions in the correction of teenagers. His sixteen-year-old daughter had just begun to date. After discussion with her, he gave her strict instructions to be in by midnight. She was twenty minutes late. Brother Merrill recalled:

"I was very tired. I had been suffering for twenty minutes

because she was late. When she came in, I immediately read her the riot act. I forgot my policies. I forgot all my positive thinking. I forgot all the great things that I knew I should do. I just simply said, ' . . . You promised to be home at 12:00. You were not home at 12:00. I worry about you. We made a call. You weren't where you said you would be. You said you would call.' And I went right down the list—bing, bing, bing, bing, negative, negative, negative, negative.

" 'Stop!' she said. . . .'We haven't been drinking, we haven't been smoking, we haven't been immoral or unchaste. We didn't go to any R-rated movie. We haven't been to a party where there were drugs. We weren't out shooting speed or doing anything else. We haven't been making out, we haven't been doing anything bad, Dad. I'm twenty minutes late for curfew, so let's keep this in perspective.' "

Brother Merrill said he fell on the floor and started to laugh, adding, "She totally shot me down because she felt that she could talk to me as a friend."[9]

That is a marvelous illustration of the importance of the scriptural direction that we only chasten and call to repentance for those actions that are sins. Of course, at some extreme point or with repetition, the violation of a well-established curfew of dating times could be a sin, though even then it probably would not be as serious as the sins it was seeking to prevent. I hope we can remember these principles in the direction and disciplining of our children.

Sometimes it is not easy to tell the difference between a mistake and a sin. The boundary can be uncertain. Take the matter of the beautiful flowering crab apple tree in our front yard. One spring when the limbs of this tree were getting too long, I pruned them, quite severely. June, my wife, evaluated my pruning and told me she thought it was a sin. I thought the extent of my pruning was a mistake at worst. I was willing to be corrected, but I did not feel I was needful of chastening and repentance.

My experience with overpruning our flowering tree leads to the observation that there is a large category of undesirable conduct that is surely an error or mistake and at an extreme level can cross over the border into transgression. When we willfully pass up an opportunity to progress toward eternal life, this is surely a mistake that should be corrected. In one way of looking at things, it is also a sin. This would apply to such things as failing to get schooling to prepare us for life, wasting our time, or failing to maintain good grooming or acquire the social or communication skills that would help us obtain employment or favorable consideration for marriage.

Mistakes can also lead to sins. The prophet Joseph Smith observed that "there are so many fools in the world for the devil to operate upon, it gives him the advantage oftentimes."[10]

The violation of special limits like curfews or missionary rules can make one vulnerable to sin. Or, a mistake committed by one person can lead another person into sin in attempting to correct it. The pruning of the flowering crab apple tree and countless other mistakes that are the subject of communication between husbands and wives and among parents and children can be mishandled to the point of producing the wrathful, angry behavior the scriptures call contention. Contention is always a transgression. This was the subject of the Apostle Paul's warning to the parents in Ephesus: "Provoke not your children to wrath: but bring them up in the nurture and admonition of the Lord" (Ephesians 6:4).

The Apostle James reminds us that "the wrath of man worketh not the righteousness of God" (James 1:20). We must be careful how we point out and correct mistakes in others, lest efforts to correct a small-sized mistake become an overreaction that produces an even larger transgression in us or in those we are attempting to help.

We should not conclude that a sin is always more serious than a mistake. Almost all sins, large and small, can be repented of, but some serious mistakes (like stepping in front of a speeding automobile) can be irreversible. This shows that a big mistake may have more serious permanent consequences than a small transgression. To cite an example more benign than a pedestrian fatality, it is a sin to be insulting or unkind to anyone, but to be insulting or unkind to your boss is a big mistake. In this case, repentance for unkindness may be easier than finding a new job for insubordination.

The Prophet Joseph Smith identified another kind of error with consequences that may be more serious than the consequences of some sins. He said that ignorance of the nature of evil spirits had caused many, including some members of the restored Church, to err in following false prophets and prophetesses. In an editorial in the *Times and Seasons,* the Prophet observed that "nothing is a greater injury to the children of men than to be under the influence of a false spirit when they think they have the Spirit of God."[11] By this account, persons innocently misled by false spirits are guilty of error and can be readily welcomed back into the fold when their error has been made known and acknowledged. That redemptive teaching rests on the scriptural distinction between errors and transgressions.

My central message is that we should always seek to distinguish between sins and mistakes in our own behavior and in the conduct of others. When we do, the scriptures direct us to the proper correction.

Sins result from willful disobedience to laws we have received by explicit teaching or by the spirit of Christ, which teaches every man the general principles of right and wrong. For sins, the remedy is to chasten and encourage repentance.

Mistakes result from ignorance of the laws of God or the workings of the universe or the people He has created. For mistakes, the remedy is to correct the mistake, not to condemn the actor.

We must make every effort to avoid sin, and to repent when

we fall short. Through the atonement of Jesus Christ we can be forgiven of our sins through repentance and baptism and by earnestly striving to keep the commandments of God. Being cleansed from sin and receiving forgiveness and reconciliation with God through the atonement of Christ is the means by which we can achieve our divine destiny as children of God.

We should seek to avoid mistakes, since some mistakes have very painful consequences. But we do not seek to avoid mistakes at all costs. Mistakes are inevitable in the process of growth in mortality. To avoid all possibility of error is to avoid all possibility of growth. In the parable of the talents, the Savior told of a servant who was so eager to minimize the risk of loss through a mistaken investment that he hid up his talent and did nothing with it. That servant was condemned by his master (Matthew 25:24–30).

If we are willing to be corrected for our mistakes—and that is a big if, since many who are mistake-prone are also correction-resistant—innocent mistakes can be a source of growth and progress. We may suffer adversities and afflictions from our own mistakes or from the mistakes of others, but in this we have a comforting promise. The Lord, who suffered for the pains and afflictions of His people (Alma 7:11; D&C 18:11, 133:53), has assured us through His prophets that He will consecrate our afflictions for our gain (2 Nephi 2:2; D&C 98:3). We can learn by experience, even from our innocent and inevitable mistakes, and our Savior will help us carry the burden of the afflictions that are inevitable in mortality. What He asks of us is to keep His commandments, to repent when we fall short, and to help and love one another as He has loved us (John 13:34).

From an address delivered at Brigham Young University on August 16, 1994, and published in the Ensign, *October 1996, 62–67.*

Notes

1. *The Abundance of the Heart,* Salt Lake City: Bookcraft, 1986, 30.
2. *Joseph Smith the Prophet,* Salt Lake City: Bookcraft, 1989, 31.
3. *Teachings of the Prophet Joseph Smith,* sel. Joseph Fielding Smith, Salt Lake City: Deseret Book, 1976, 193.
4. *Teachings of the Prophet Joseph Smith,* 240–41.
5. Walter Savage Landor, in *Bartlett's Familiar Quotations,* ed. Justin Kaplan, 16th ed., Boston: Little, Brown, 1992, 388.
6. "Prophet Focuses on Christ's Message," *Church News,* 9 July 1994, 3.
7. *Journal of Discourses,* 26 vols., London: Latter-day Saints' Book Depot, 1854–86, 13:346.
8. *General Handbook of Instructions,* 2 vols., Salt Lake City: The Church of Jesus Christ of Latter-day Saints, 1998, 1:96.
9. "Building Your Child's Self-Esteem," *Families Are Forever,* VISN cable network, 1989.
10. *Teachings of the Prophet Joseph Smith,* 331.
11. *History of The Church of Jesus Christ of Latter-day Saints,* ed. B. H. Roberts, 2d ed. rev., 7 vols., Salt Lake City: The Church of Jesus Christ of Latter-day Saints, 1932–51.

15

REVELATION

REVELATION IS COMMUNICATION from God to man. It can occur in many different ways. Some prophets, like Moses and Joseph Smith, have talked with God face-to-face. Some persons have had personal communication with angels. Others have received revelations, as Elder James E. Talmage observed, "through the dreams of sleep or in the waking visions of the mind."[1]

In its more familiar forms, revelation or inspiration comes by means of words or thoughts communicated to the mind (D&C 8:2–3; Enos 1:10), by sudden enlightenment (D&C 6:14–15), by positive or negative feelings about proposed courses of action, or even by inspiring performances, such as in the performing arts. As Elder Boyd K. Packer has stated, "Inspiration comes more as a feeling than as a sound."[2]

I have chosen to discuss this subject in terms of a different classification according to the purpose of the communication. I can identify eight different purposes served by communication from God: (1) to testify; (2) to prophesy; (3) to comfort; (4) to uplift; (5) to inform; (6) to restrain; (7) to confirm; and (8) to impel. I will describe each of these in that order, giving examples.

My purpose in suggesting this classification and in giving these examples is to persuade each of you to search your own experience and to conclude that you have already received revelations and that you can receive more revelations because communication from God to men and women is a reality. President Lorenzo Snow declared that it is "the grand privilege of every Latter-day Saint . . . to have the manifestations of the spirit every day of our lives."[3] President Harold B. Lee taught:

"Every man has the privilege to exercise these gifts and these privileges in the conduct of his own affairs; in bringing up his children in the way they should go; in the management of his business, or whatever he does. It is his right to enjoy the spirit of revelation and of inspiration to do the right thing, to be wise and prudent, just and good, in everything that he does."[4]

As I review the following eight purposes of revelation, I hope you will recognize the extent to which you have already received revelation or inspiration, and resolve to cultivate this spiritual gift for more frequent use in the future.

Purposes of Revelation

1. The testimony or witness of the Holy Ghost that Jesus is the Christ and that the gospel is true is a revelation from God. When the Apostle Peter affirmed that Jesus Christ was the Son of the living God, the Savior called him blessed, "for flesh and blood have not revealed it unto thee, but my Father which is in heaven" (Matthew 16:17). This precious revelation can be part of the personal experience of every seeker after truth and, once received, becomes a polestar to guide in all the activities of life.

2. Prophecy is another purpose or function of revelation. Speaking under the influence of the Holy Ghost and within the limits of our stewardship, we may be inspired to predict what will come to pass in the future. This is the office of the Prophet, Seer, and Revelator, who prophesies for the Church, as Joseph Smith prophesied the Civil War (D&C 87) and foretold that the Saints would become a mighty people in the Rocky Mountains.[5] Prophecy is part of the calling of an ordained patriarch.

Each of us is privileged to receive prophetic revelation illuminating future events in our lives, such as a Church calling we are to receive. To cite another example, after our fifth child was born, my wife and I did not have any more children. After more than ten years, we concluded that our family would not be any larger, which grieved us. Then one day, while my wife was in the temple, the Spirit whispered to her that she would have another child. That prophetic revelation was fulfilled a year and a half later with the birth of our sixth child, for whom we had waited thirteen years.

3. A third purpose of revelation is to give comfort. Such a revelation came to the Prophet Joseph Smith in Liberty Jail. After many months in deplorable conditions, he cried out in agony and loneliness, pleading with the Lord to remember the persecuted Saints. The comforting answer came:

"My son, peace be unto thy soul; thine adversity and thine afflictions shall be but a small moment; and then, if thou endure it well, God shall exalt thee on high; thou shalt triumph over all thy foes" (D&C 121:7–8).

In that same revelation the Lord declared that, no matter what tragedies or injustices should befall the Prophet, "Know thou, my son, that all these things shall give thee experience, and shall be for thy good" (D&C 122:7).

Each of us knows of other examples of revelations of comfort. Some have been comforted by visions of departed loved ones or by feeling their presence. The widow of a good friend told me how she had felt the presence of her departed husband, giving her assurance of his love and concern for her. Others have been comforted in adjusting to the loss of a job or a business advantage or even a marriage. A revelation of comfort can also come in connection with a blessing of the priesthood, either from the words spoken or from the feeling communicated in connection with the blessing.

Another type of comforting revelation is the assurance received that a sin has been forgiven. After praying fervently for an entire day and night, a Book of Mormon prophet recorded that he heard a voice, which said, "Thy sins are forgiven thee, and thou shalt be blessed." As a result, Enos wrote, "My guilt was swept away" (Enos 1:5–6; D&C 61:2). This assurance, which comes when a person has completed all the steps of repentance, gives assurance that the price has been paid, that God has heard the repentant sinner, and that the sinner's sins are forgiven.

Alma described that moment as a time when he was no longer "harrowed up by the memory" of his sins. "And oh, what joy, and what marvelous light I did behold; yea, my soul was filled with joy . . . there can be nothing so exquisite and sweet as was my joy" (Alma 36:19–21).

4. Closely related to the feeling of comfort is the fourth purpose or function of revelation: to uplift. At some time in our lives, each of us needs to be lifted from a depression, from a sense of foreboding or inadequacy, or just from a plateau of spiritual mediocrity. Because the feeling of uplift raises our spirits and helps us resist evil and seek good, I believe that the uplift communicated by reading the scriptures and enjoying wholesome music, art, or literature is a distinct purpose of revelation.

5. The fifth purpose of revelation is to inform. This may consist of inspiration giving a person the words to speak on a particular occasion, such as in the blessings pronounced by an ordained patriarch or in sermons or other words spoken under the

influence of the Holy Ghost. The Lord commanded Joseph Smith and Sidney Rigdon to lift their voices and speak the thoughts that He would put in their hearts, "For it shall be given you in the very hour, yea, in the very moment, what ye shall say" (D&C 100:5–6; 84:85; 124:97).

On some sacred occasions, information has been given by face-to-face conversations with heavenly personages, such as in the visions related in ancient and modern scriptures. In other circumstances, needed information is communicated by the quiet whisperings of the Spirit. A child loses a treasured possession, prays for help, and is inspired to find it; an adult has a problem at work, at home, or in genealogical research, prays, and is led to the information necessary to resolve it; a Church leader prays to know whom the Lord would have him call to fill a position, and the Spirit whispers a name. In all of these examples—familiar to each of us—the Holy Ghost acts in his office as a teacher and revelator, communicating information and truths for the edification and guidance of the recipient.

Revelation from God serves all five of these purposes: testimony, prophecy, comfort, uplift, and information. I have mentioned them only briefly, giving examples principally from the scriptures. I will discuss at greater length the remaining three purposes of revelation, giving examples from my personal experience.

6. The sixth type or purpose of revelation is to restrain us from doing something. Thus, in the midst of a great sermon explaining the power of the Holy Ghost, Nephi suddenly declared, "And now I . . . cannot say more; the Spirit stoppeth mine utterance" (2 Nephi 32:7). The revelation that restrains is one of the most common forms of revelation. It often comes by surprise, when we have not asked for revelation or guidance on a particular subject. But if we are keeping the commandments of God and living in tune with His Spirit, a restraining force will steer us away from things we should not do.

One of my first experiences in being restrained by the Spirit came soon after I was called as a counselor in a stake presidency in Chicago. In one of our first presidency meetings, our stake president made a proposal that our new stake center be built in a particular location. I immediately saw four or five good reasons that the proposed location was wrong. When asked for my counsel, I opposed the proposal, giving each of those reasons. The stake president wisely proposed that each of us consider the matter prayerfully for another week and discuss it further in our next meeting. Almost perfunctorily I prayed about the subject and immediately received a strong impression that I was wrong, that I was standing in the way of the Lord's will, and that I should remove myself from opposition to it.

Needless to say, I was restrained and promptly gave my approval to the proposed construction. Incidentally, the wisdom of constructing the stake center in that location was soon evident, even to me. My reasons to the contrary turned out to be short-sighted, and I was soon grateful to have been restrained from relying on them.

Many years ago I picked up the desk pen in my office at Brigham Young University to sign a paper that had been prepared for my signature, something I did at least a dozen times each day. That document committed the university to a particular course of action we had decided to follow. All the staff work had been done, and all appeared to be in order. But as I went to sign the document, I was filled with such negative thoughts and forebodings that I put it to one side and asked for the entire matter to be reviewed again. It was, and within a few days additional facts came to light which showed that the proposed course of action would have caused the university serious problems in the future.

On another occasion, the Spirit came to my assistance as I was editing a casebook on a legal subject. A casebook consists of several hundred court opinions, together with explanatory material and text written by the editor. My assistant and I had finished all the work on the book, including the necessary research to assure that these court opinions had not been reversed or overruled. Just before sending it to the publisher, I was leafing through the manuscript, and a particular court opinion caught my attention. As I looked at it, I had a profoundly uneasy feeling. I asked my assistant to check that opinion again to see if everything was in order. He did and reported that it was.

In a subsequent check of the completed manuscript, I was again stopped at that case, again with a great feeling of uneasiness. This time I went to the law library myself. There, in some newly received publications, I discovered that this case had just been reversed on appeal. If that opinion had been published in my casebook, it would have been a serious professional embarrassment. I was saved by the restraining power of revelation.

7. A common way to seek revelation is to propose a particular course of action and then pray for inspiration to confirm it. The Lord explained the confirming type of revelation when Oliver Cowdery failed in his efforts to translate the Book of Mormon: "Behold, you have not understood; you have supposed that I would give it unto you, when you took no thought save it was to ask me. But, behold, I say unto you, that you must study it out in your mind; then you must ask me if it be right, and if it is right I will cause that your bosom shall burn within you; therefore, you shall feel that it is right" (D&C 9:7–8).

Similarly, the prophet Alma likened the word of God to a seed and told gospel investigators that if they would give place for the seed to be planted in their hearts, the seed would enlarge their souls, enlighten their understanding, and begin to be delicious to them (Alma 32). That feeling is the Holy Ghost's confirming revelation of the truth of the word.

When he spoke on the Brigham Young University campus some years ago on the subject "agency or inspiration," Elder Bruce R. McConkie stressed our responsibility to do all we can before we seek a revelation. He gave a very personal example. When he set out to choose a companion for eternity, he did not go to the Lord and ask whom he ought to marry. "I went out and found the girl I wanted," he said. "She suited me; . . . it just seemed . . . as though this ought to be. . . . [Then] all I did was pray to the Lord and ask for some guidance and direction in connection with the decision that I'd reached."[6]

Elder McConkie summarized his counsel on the balance between agency and inspiration in these sentences:

"We're expected to use the gifts and talents and abilities, the sense and judgment and agency with which we are endowed. . . . Implicit in asking in faith is the precedent requirement that we do everything in our power to accomplish the goal that we seek. . . . We're expected to do everything in our power that we can, and then to seek an answer from the Lord, a confirming seal that we've reached the right conclusion."[7]

As a regional representative, I was privileged to work with four different members of the Quorum of the Twelve and with other General Authorities as they sought revelation in connection with the calling of stake presidents. All proceeded in the same manner. They interviewed persons residing in the stake— counselors in the stake presidency, members of the high council, bishops, and others who had gained special experience in Church administration—asking them questions and hearing their counsel. As they conducted these interviews, the servants of the Lord gave prayerful consideration to each person interviewed and men- tioned. Finally, they reached a tentative decision on the new stake president. This proposal was then prayerfully submitted to the Lord. If it was confirmed, the call was issued. If it was not con- firmed, or if they were restrained, that proposal was tabled, and the process continued until a new proposal was formed and the confirming revelation was received.

Sometimes confirming and restraining revelations are combined. For example, during my service at Brigham Young

University, I was invited to give a speech before a national association of attorneys. I had routinely declined this kind of speaking invitation because it would require many days to prepare. But as I began to dictate a letter declining this particular invitation, I felt restrained. I paused and reconsidered my action. I then considered how I might accept it, and as I came to consider the invitation in that light, I felt the confirming assurance of the Spirit and knew that I must accept it.

The speech that resulted, "A Private University Looks at Government Regulation," opened the door to a host of important opportunities. I was invited to repeat that same speech before several other nationally prominent groups. It was published in *Vital Speeches,* in a professional journal, and in several other periodicals and books, from which it was used as a leading statement of the private university's interest in freedom from government regulation. This speech led to Brigham Young University's being consulted by various church groups on the proper relationship between government and a church-related college. These consultations in turn contributed to the formation of a national organization of church-related colleges and universities that has provided a significant coalition to oppose unlawful or unwise government regulation.

I have no doubt, as I look back on the event, that this speech I almost declined to give was one of those occasions when a seemingly insignificant act made a great deal of difference. Those are the times when it is vital for us to receive the guidance of the Lord, and those are the times when revelation will come to aid us if we hear and heed it.

8. The eighth purpose or type of revelation consists of those instances when the Spirit impels a person to action. This is not a case in which a person proposes to take a particular action and the Spirit either restrains or confirms. This is a case in which revelation comes when it is not being sought and impels some action not

proposed. This type of revelation is obviously less common than other types, but its rarity makes it all the more significant.

A scriptural example is recorded in the first book of Nephi. When Nephi was in Jerusalem to obtain the precious records from the treasury, the Spirit of the Lord directed him to kill Laban as he lay drunk in the street. This act was so far from Nephi's heart that he recoiled and wrestled with the Spirit, but he was again directed to slay Laban, and he finally followed that revelation (1 Nephi 4).

Students of Church history will recall Wilford Woodruff's account of an impression that came to him in the night telling him to move his carriage and mules away from a large tree. He did so, and his family and livestock were saved when the tree crashed to the ground in a whirlwind that struck thirty minutes later.[8]

As a young girl, my grandmother, Chasty Olsen Harris, had a similar experience. She was tending some children who were playing in a dry riverbed near their home in Castle Dale, Utah. Suddenly she heard a voice that called her by name and directed her to get the children out of the riverbed and up on the bank. It was a clear day, and there was no sign of rain. She saw no reason to heed the voice and continued to play. The voice spoke to her again, urgently. This time she heeded the warning. Quickly gathering the children, she made a run for the bank. Just as they reached it, an enormous wall of water, originating with a cloudburst in the mountains many miles away, swept down the canyon and roared across where the children had played. Except for this impelling revelation, she and the children would have been lost.

For nine years Professor Marvin S. Hill and I had worked on the book *Carthage Conspiracy*, which concerns the 1845 court trial of the murderers of Joseph Smith. We had several different sources of minutes on the trial, some bearing their authors' names and others unsigned. The fullest set of minutes was unsigned, but because we had located them in the Church Historian's Office, we were sure they were the minutes kept by George Watt, the

Church's official scribe who was sent to record the proceedings of the trial. We so stated in seven drafts of our manuscript, and we analyzed all our sources on that assumption.

Finally, the book was completed, and within a few weeks the final manuscript would be sent to the publisher. As I sat in my office one Saturday afternoon, I felt impelled to go through a pile of unexamined books and pamphlets accumulated on the table behind my desk. At the very bottom of the pile of fifty or sixty publications, I found a printed catalog of the contents of the Wilford C. Wood Museum, which Professor LaMar Berrett, the author, had sent to me a year and a half earlier.

As I quickly flipped through the pages of this catalog of Church history manuscripts, my eyes fell on a page describing the manuscript of the trial minutes we had attributed to George Watt. This catalog page told how Wilford Wood had purchased the original of that set of minutes in Illinois and had given the Church a typewritten version, the same version we had obtained from the church historian. We immediately visited the Wilford Wood Museum in Woods Cross, Utah, and obtained additional information that enabled us to determine that the minutes we had thought were the official Church source had actually been prepared by one of the lawyers for the defense.

With this knowledge, we returned to the Church Historian's Office and were able to locate for the first time George Watt's official and highly authentic set of minutes on the trial. This discovery saved us from a grievous error in the identification of one of our major sources and also permitted us to enrich the contents of our book significantly. The impression I received that day in my office was a cherished example of the way the Lord will help us in our righteous professional pursuits when we qualify for the impressions of His Spirit.

I had another choice experience with impelling revelation a few months after I began my service at Brigham Young University. As a new and inexperienced president, I had many problems to analyze and many decisions to reach. I was very dependent on the Lord. One day in October, I drove up Provo Canyon to ponder a particular problem. Although alone and without any interruption, I found myself unable to think of the problem at hand. Another pending issue I was not yet ready to consider kept thrusting itself into my mind: Should we modify the university's academic calendar to complete the fall semester before Christmas?

After ten or fifteen minutes of unsuccessful efforts to exclude thoughts of this subject, I finally realized what was happening. The issue of the calendar did not seem timely to me, and I was certainly not seeking any guidance on it, but the Spirit was trying to communicate with me on that subject. I immediately turned my full attention to that question and began to record my thoughts on a piece of paper. Within a few minutes, I had recorded the details of a three-semester calendar, with all of its powerful advantages. Hurrying back to the campus, I reviewed it with my colleagues and found them enthusiastic. A few days later the Board of Trustees approved our proposed new calendar, and we published its dates, barely in time to make them effective in the fall of 1972. Since that time, I have reread the following words of the Prophet Joseph Smith and realized that I had the experience he described:

"A person may profit by noticing the first intimation of the spirit of revelation; for instance, when you feel pure intelligence flowing into you, it may give you sudden strokes of ideas . . . and thus by learning the Spirit of God and understanding it, you may grow into the principle of revelation."[9]

Revelations Not Received

I have described eight different purposes or types of revelation: (1) testifying, (2) prophesying, (3) comforting, (4) uplifting, (5) informing, (6) restraining, (7) confirming, and (8) impelling. Each of these refers to revelations that are received. I now wish to suggest a few ideas about revelations that are not received.

First, we should understand what can be called the principle of "stewardship in revelation." Our Heavenly Father's house is a house of order, where His servants are commanded to "act in the office in which [they are] appointed" (D&C 107:99). This principle applies to revelation. Only the president of the Church receives revelation to guide the entire Church. Only the stake president receives revelation for the special guidance of the stake. The person who receives revelation for the ward is the bishop. For a family, it is the priesthood leadership (parents) of the family.

Leaders receive revelation for their own stewardships. Individuals can receive revelation to guide their own lives. But when one person purports to receive revelation for another person outside his or her own stewardship—such as a Church member who claims to have revelation to guide the entire Church or a person who claims to have a revelation to guide another person over whom he or she has no presiding authority according to the order of the Church—you can be sure that such revelations are not from the Lord. Elder Boyd K. Packer has called such revelations "counterfeit signals."[10]

Satan is a great deceiver, and he is the source of some of these spurious revelations. Others are simply imagined. If a revelation is outside the limits of stewardship, you know it is not from the Lord, and you are not bound by it. I have heard of cases in which a young man tells a young woman that she should marry him because he has received a revelation that she is to be his eternal companion. If this is a true revelation, it will be confirmed directly to the woman if she seeks to know. In the meantime, she is under no obligation to heed it. She should seek her own guidance and make up her own mind. The man can receive revelation to guide his own actions, but he cannot properly receive revelation to direct hers. She is outside his stewardship.

What about those times when we seek revelation and do not

receive it? We do not always receive inspiration or revelation when we request it. Sometimes we are delayed in the receipt of revelation, and sometimes we are left to our own judgment. We cannot force spiritual things. It must be so. Our life's purpose to obtain experience and to develop faith would be frustrated if our Heavenly Father directed us in every act, even in every important act. We must make decisions and experience the consequences in order to develop self-reliance and faith.

Even in decisions we think very important, we sometimes receive no answers to our prayers. This does not mean that our prayers have not been heard. It only means that we have prayed about a decision which, for one reason or another, we should make without guidance by revelation. Perhaps we have asked for guidance in choosing between alternatives that are equally acceptable or equally unacceptable.

I suggest that there is not a right and wrong to every question. To many questions, there are only two wrong answers or two right answers. Thus, a person who seeks guidance on which of two different ways he should pursue to get even with a person who has wronged him is not likely to receive revelation. Neither is a person who seeks guidance on a choice he will never have to make because some future event will intervene, such as a third alternative that is clearly preferable.

On one occasion, my wife and I prayed earnestly for guidance on a decision that seemed very important. No answer came. We were left to proceed on our own best judgment. We could not imagine why the Lord had not aided us with a confirming or restraining impression. But it was not long before we learned that we did not have to make a decision on that question because something else happened that made a decision unnecessary. The Lord would not guide us in a selection that made no difference.

No answer is likely to come to a person who seeks guidance in choosing between two alternatives that are equally acceptable to the Lord. Thus, there are times when we can serve productively in two different fields of labor. Either choice is right. Similarly, the Spirit of the Lord is not likely to give us revelations on matters that are trivial. I once heard a young woman in a testimony meeting praise the spirituality of her husband, indicating that he submitted every question to the Lord. She told how he accompanied her shopping and would not even choose between different brands of canned vegetables without making his selection a matter of prayer. That strikes me as improper. I believe the Lord expects us to use the intelligence and experience He has given us to make these kinds of choices. When a member asked the Prophet Joseph Smith for advice on particular matter, the Prophet stated:

"It is a great thing to inquire at the hands of God, or to come into His presence; and we feel fearful to approach Him on subjects that are of little or no consequence."[11]

Of course we are not always able to judge what is trivial. If a matter appears of little or no consequence, we can proceed on the basis of our own judgment. If the choice is important for reasons unknown to us, such as the speaking invitation I mentioned earlier or even a choice between two cans of vegetables when one contains a hidden poison, the Lord will intervene and give us guidance. When a choice will make a real difference in our lives—obvious or not—and when we are living in tune with the Spirit and seeking God's guidance, we can be sure we will receive the guidance we need to attain our goal. The Lord will not leave us unassisted when a choice is important to our eternal welfare.

I know that God lives and that revelation to His children is a reality. I pray that we will be worthy and willing, and that He will bless us to grow in this principle of revelation.

———————————

From an address delivered at Brigham Young University on September 29, 1981, and published in abbreviated form in the New Era, *September 1982, 38–46; for further discussion pertaining to revelation, see the author's* The Lord's Way, *22–32.*

NOTES

1. *Articles of Faith,* Salt Lake City: Deseret Book, 1984, 229.
2. "Prayers and Answers," *Ensign,* November 1979, 19.
3. In Conference Report, April 1899, 52.
4. *Stand Ye in Holy Places,* Salt Lake City: Deseret Book, 1974, 141–42.
5. *Teachings of the Prophet Joseph Smith,* comp. Joseph Fielding Smith, Salt Lake City: Deseret Book, 1976, 255.
6. "Agency or Inspiration—Which?" *BYU Speeches of the Year, 1972–73,* Provo, Utah: Brigham Young University Press, 1973, 111.
7. "Agency or Inspiration—Which?" 108, 110, 113.
8. Matthias F. Cowley, *Wilford Woodruff: History of His Life and Labors,* Salt Lake City: Bookcraft, 1964, 131–32.
9. *Teachings of the Prophet Joseph Smith,* 151.
10. "Prayers and Answers," *Ensign,* November 1979, 20.
11. *Teachings of the Prophet Joseph Smith,* 22.

16

OUR STRENGTHS CAN BECOME OUR DOWNFALL

THE LORD WARNED THE FIRST generation of Latter-day Saints to "beware concerning yourselves" (D&C 84:43). That warning provides a preamble to this reminder of the mortal susceptibilities and the devilish diversions that can unite to produce our spiritual downfall.

Lehi taught that "it must needs be, that there is an opposition in all things. If not so, . . . righteousness could not be brought to pass" (2 Nephi 2:11). In the realm of spiritual progress, that opposition is provided by the temptations of Satan. We learn in modern revelation that "it must needs be that the devil should tempt the children of men, or they could not be agents unto themselves" (D&C 29:39).

President Romney taught, "Latter-day Saints know that there is a God. With like certainty, they know that Satan lives, that he is a powerful personage of spirit, the archenemy of God, of man, and of righteousness." He then described one of Satan's methods: "Satan is a skillful imitator, and as genuine gospel truth is given the world in ever-increasing abundance, so he spreads the counterfeit coin of false doctrine."[1]

Satan uses every possible device to accomplish his purpose to degrade and enslave every soul. He attempts to distort and corrupt everything created for the good of man, sometimes by diluting that which is good, sometimes by camouflaging that which is evil.

We generally think of Satan attacking us at our weakest spot. President Kimball described this technique when he said, "Lucifer and his followers know the habits, weaknesses, and vulnerable spots of everyone and take advantage of them to lead us to spiritual destruction."[2]

Like the fabled Achilles, who was immune to every lethal blow except to his heel, many of us have a special weakness that can be exploited to our spiritual downfall. For some, that weakness may be a taste for liquor or a craving for money or power. For others, it may be an unusual vulnerability to sexual temptation or a susceptibility to compulsive gambling or reckless speculation. If we are wise, we will know our special weaknesses, our spiritual Achilles heels, and fortify ourselves against temptations in those areas.

But our weaknesses are not the only areas where we are vulnerable. Satan can also attack us where we think we are strong—in the very areas where we are proud of our strengths. He will approach us through the greatest talents and spiritual gifts we possess. If we are not wary, Satan can cause our spiritual downfall by corrupting us through our strengths as well as by exploiting our weaknesses. I will illustrate this truth with a score of examples.

1. My first example concerns Satan's efforts to corrupt a person who has an unusual commitment to one particular doctrine or commandment of the gospel of Jesus Christ. This could be an unusual talent for family history work, an extraordinary

commitment to constitutional government, a special talent in the acquisition of knowledge, or any other special talent or commitment.

In a memorable message given at the October 1971 general conference, Elder Boyd K. Packer likened the fullness of the gospel to a piano keyboard. He reminded us that people could be "attracted by a single key," such as a doctrine they want to hear "played over and over again." He explained:

"Some members of the Church who should know better pick out a hobby key or two and tap them incessantly, to the irritation of those around them. They can dull their own spiritual sensitivities. They lose track that there is a fulness of the gospel, . . . [which they reject] in preference to a favorite note. This becomes exaggerated and distorted, leading them away into apostasy."[3]

We could say of such persons, as the Lord said of the members of the Shaker sect in a revelation given in 1831, "Behold, I say unto you, that they desire to know the truth in part, but not all" (D&C 49:2). And so I say, beware of a hobby key. If you tap one key to the exclusion or serious detriment of the full harmony of the gospel keyboard, Satan can use your strength to bring you down.

2. Satan will also attempt to cause our spiritual downfall through tempting us to misapply our spiritual gifts. The revelations tell us that "there are many gifts, and to every man is given a gift by the Spirit of God" (D&C 46:11). All of these gifts "come from God, for the benefit of the children of God" (D&C 46:26). Most of us have seen persons whom the adversary has led astray through a corruption of their spiritual gifts. My mother shared one such example, something she had observed while she was a college student many years ago.

A man who lived in a community in Utah had a mighty gift of healing. People sought him out for blessings, many coming from outside his ward and stake. In time, he made almost a profession of giving blessings. As part of his travels to various communities, he came to the apartments of Brigham Young University students, asking if they wanted blessings. This man had lost sight of the revealed direction on spiritual gifts: "always remembering for what they are given" (D&C 46:8). A spiritual gift is given to benefit the children of God, not to magnify the prominence or gratify the ego of the person who receives it. The professional healer who forgot that lesson gradually lost the companionship of the Spirit and was eventually excommunicated from the Church.

3. Another strength Satan can exploit to seek our downfall is a strong desire to understand everything about every principle of the gospel. How could that possibly work to our detriment? Experience teaches that if this desire is not disciplined, it can cause some to pursue their searchings past the fringes of orthodoxy, seeking answers to mysteries rather than a firmer understanding and a better practice of the basic principles of the gospel.

Some seek answers to questions God has not chosen to answer. Others receive answers—or think they receive answers—in ways that are contrary to the order of the Church. For such searchers, Satan stands ready to mislead through sophistry, or spurious revelation. Persons who hunger after a full understanding of all things must discipline their questions and their methods or they can get close to apostasy without even knowing it. It may be just as dangerous to exceed orthodoxy as it is to fall short of it. The safety and happiness we are promised lies in keeping the commandments, not in discounting them or multiplying them.

4. Closely related to this example is the person who has a strong desire to be led by the Spirit of the Lord but who unwisely extends that strength to the point of desiring to be led in all things. A desire to be led by the Lord is a strength, but it needs to be accompanied by an understanding that our Heavenly Father leaves many decisions for our personal choices. Personal decision making is one of the sources of the growth we are meant to experience in mortality. Persons who try to shift all decision making

to the Lord and plead for revelation in every choice will soon find circumstances in which they pray for guidance and do not receive it. For example, this is likely to occur in those numerous circumstances when the choices are trivial or when either choice is acceptable. We should study things out in our minds using the reasoning powers our Creator has placed within us. Then we should pray for guidance and act upon it if we receive it; if we do not receive guidance, we should act upon our best judgment.

Persons who persist in seeking revelatory guidance on subjects on which the Lord has not chosen to direct us may concoct an answer out of their own fantasy or bias, or they may even receive an answer through the medium of false revelation. Revelation from God is a sacred reality, but like other sacred things it must be cherished and used properly so that a great strength does not become a disabling weakness.

5. The honors we sometimes receive from our peers are potentially a strength, but we need to remember that Satan can turn these to our detriment also. We must be careful that we do not become like the Prophet Balaam. The Apostle Peter said that Balaam "loved the wages of unrighteousness" (2 Peter 2:15), which Elder McConkie interpreted as "the honors of men and the wealth of the world."4 Honors may come, but we should beware that they not deflect our priorities and commitments away from the things of God.

6. A willingness to sacrifice all we possess in the work of the Lord is surely a strength. In fact, it is a covenant we make in sacred places. But even this strength can bring us down if we fail to confine our sacrifices to those things the Lord and His leaders have asked of us at this time. We should say with Alma, "Why should I desire more than to perform the work to which I have been called?" (Alma 29:6). Persons who consider it insufficient to pay their tithes and offerings and to work in the positions to which they have been called can easily be led astray by cultist groups and other bizarre outlets for their willingness to sacrifice.

7. Some persons have a finely developed social conscience. They respond to social injustice and suffering with great concern, commitment, and generosity. This is surely a spiritual strength, something many of us need in greater measure. Yet persons who have this great quality need to be cautious that it not impel them to overstep other ultimate values.

My social conscience should not cause me to coerce others to use their time or means to fulfill my objectives. We are not blessed for magnifying our calling with someone else's time or resources. We are commanded to *love* our neighbors, not to *manipulate* them, even for righteous purposes. In the same way, we should not feel alienated from our Church or its leaders when they refrain from using the rhetoric of the social gospel or from allocating Church resources to purposes favored by others.

We should remember that the Lord has given His restored Church a unique mission not given to others. We must concentrate our primary efforts on those activities that can only be accomplished with priesthood authority, such as preaching the gospel and redeeming the dead.

8. There is great strength in being highly focused on our goals. We have all seen the favorable fruits of that focus. Yet an intense focus on goals can cause a person to forget the importance of righteous *means.* When I was serving in a stake presidency, a man bragged to me about the way he had managed to preserve his goal of perfect attendance at our stake leadership meetings. He was required to report for his shift work at the time of one of our stake meetings. When the employer denied his request for permission to attend this church meeting, he told me with pride that he "called in sick" so he could come anyway. I kept an eye on that man after that. I wondered if he would steal money in order to pay his tithing. That may be an extreme example, but it illustrates the point I wish to make. We cannot be so concerned about our goals that we overlook the necessity of using righteous methods to attain them.

9. Another illustration of a strength that can become our downfall concerns the charismatic teacher. With a trained mind and a skillful manner of presentation, a teacher can become unusually popular and effective in teaching. But Satan will try to use that strength to corrupt the teacher by encouraging him or her to gather a following of disciples. A church or church education teacher or LDS university professor who gathers such a following and does this "for the sake of riches and honor" (Alma 1:16) is guilty of priestcraft. "Priestcrafts are that men preach and set themselves up for a light unto the world, that they may get gain and praise of the world; but they seek not the welfare of Zion" (2 Nephi 26:29).

Teachers who are most popular (and therefore most effective) have a special susceptibility to this form of priestcraft. If they are not careful, their strength can become their spiritual downfall. They can become like Almon Babbitt, with whom the Lord was not pleased because, the revelation states, "he aspireth to establish his counsel instead of the counsel which I have ordained, even that of the Presidency of my Church; and he setteth up a golden calf for the worship of my people" (D&C 124:84).

10. The family, the most sacred institution in mortality, is a setting in which Satan is especially eager to use strengths to bring about our downfall. My first illustration under this heading is addressed to breadwinners. The Bible says that it is a gift of God to rejoice in our labors (Ecclesiastes 5:19). But that strength can be corrupted. Our labors, and the prosperity and recognition we achieve by them, can easily become a god we place before Him who said, "Thou shalt have no other gods before me" (Exodus 20:3). Carried to excess, a love of and commitment to work can also become an excuse to neglect family and church responsibilities. Most of us could cite more than one illustration of that reality.

11. At an even more sensitive level, a man's righteous desire to act in his position as a leader in his family, if not righteously

exercised, can lead him into self-righteousness, selfishness, dictatorship, and even brutality. A timely warning against this danger is the Lord's blunt instruction "that it is the nature and disposition" of those who have a little authority to "exercise unrighteous dominion." We must all heed the direction that priesthood authority must be exercised "by persuasion, by long-suffering, by gentleness and meekness, and by love unfeigned" (D&C 121: 39, 41).

12. By the same token, a woman's righteous and appropriate desires to grow and develop and magnify her talents—desires strongly reinforced by current feminist teachings—also have their extreme manifestations. Such manifestations can lead to attempts to preempt priesthood leadership, to the advocacy of ideas out of harmony with Church doctrine, or even to the abandonment of family responsibilities.

13. Another area in which strengths can become our downfall concerns finances. We are commanded to give to the poor. Could the fulfillment of that fundamental Christian obligation be carried to excess? I believe it can, and I believe I have seen examples of this. Perhaps you have also seen cases where persons fulfilled that duty to such an extent that they impoverished their own families by expending resources or property or time that were needed for family members.

Perhaps this excess explains why King Benjamin, who commanded his people to impart of their substance to the poor, "feeding the hungry, clothing the naked, visiting the sick and administering to their relief, both spiritually and temporally," also cautioned them to "see that all these things are done in wisdom and order; for it is not requisite that a man should run faster than he has strength" (Mosiah 4:26–27). Similarly, a revelation given to the Prophet Joseph Smith during the time he was translating the Book of Mormon cautioned him, "Do not run faster or labor more than you have strength and means provided to enable you to translate" (D&C 10:4).

14. A desire to know is surely a great strength. A hunger to learn is laudable, but the fruits of learning make a person particularly susceptible to the sin of pride. So do the fruits of other talents and accomplishments, such as the athletic or the artistic. It is easy for the learned and the accomplished to forget their own limitations and their total dependence upon God.

Accomplishments in higher education bring persons much recognition and real feelings of self-sufficiency. But we should remember the Book of Mormon's frequent cautions not to boast in our own strength or wisdom lest we be left to our own strength or wisdom (Alma 38:11, 39:2; Helaman 4:13, 16:15). Similarly, the prophet Jacob referred to "that cunning plan of the evil one," remarking that when persons are "learned," which means that they have knowledge, "they think they are wise," which means that they think they have the capacity for the wise application of knowledge. Persons who think they are wise in this way "hearken not unto the counsel of God, for they set it aside, supposing they know of themselves." In that circumstance, the prophet said, "their wisdom is foolishness and it profiteth them not. And they shall perish. To be learned is good," the word of the Lord concludes, "if they hearken unto the counsels of God" (2 Nephi 9:28–29).

15. An unusual degree of faith in God, a genuine spiritual gift and strength, can be distorted so as to seriously detract from scholarly pursuits. I have known persons who began their academic studies with great momentum, but as time went by did not continue to invest the time they needed in their studies because they supposed they had developed such great faith that if they simply did their church work the Lord would bless them to achieve their academic objectives. In this way, the supposed strength of their faith became the cause of their academic downfall. We might say to them as the Lord said to Oliver Cowdery when he failed in his efforts to translate:

"Behold, it is because that you did not continue as you

commenced. . . . You have supposed that I would give it unto you, when you took no thought save it was to ask me. But, behold, I say unto you, that you must study it out in your mind; then you must ask me if it be right" (D&C 9:5, 7–8).

Here the Lord counsels us on balance. Faith is vital, but it must be accompanied by the personal work appropriate to the task. Only then do we qualify for the blessing. The appropriate approach for students is to study as if everything depended upon them and then to pray and exercise faith as if everything depended upon the Lord.

16. A related strength that can be corrupted to the downfall of a student is a desire to excel in a Church calling. I remember a graduate student who used his church service as a means of escape from the rigors of his studies. He went beyond what we call church-service time and became almost a full-time church-service worker, consistently volunteering for every extra assignment and giving help that was greatly appreciated in the various organizations and activities of the Church, but finally failing in his studies and blaming his failure on the excessive burden of his church work. His strength became his downfall.

Similarly, I remember the concerns President Harold B. Lee expressed to me when I was president of Brigham Young University. Shortly before the Provo Utah Temple was dedicated, he told me of his concern that the accessibility of the temple would cause some students to attend the temple so often that they would neglect their studies. He urged me to work with Brigham Young University stake presidents to make sure that the students understood that even something as sacred and important as temple service needed to be done in wisdom and order so that the students would not neglect the studies that should be the major focus of their time during their student years.

17. Love of country is surely a strength, but carried to excess it can become the cause of spiritual downfall. Patriotism as defined by some citizens is so intense and so all-consuming that it

seems to override every other responsibility, including family and Church responsibilities. For example, I caution those patriots who are participating in or provisioning private armies and making private preparations for armed conflict. Their excessive zeal for one aspect of patriotism is causing them to risk spiritual downfall as they withdraw from the society of the Church and from the governance of those civil authorities to whom our twelfth article of faith makes all of us subject.

18. Another strength that can become our downfall stems from self-reliance. We are told to be self-reliant and to provide for ourselves and those dependent upon us. But success at that effort can easily escalate into materialism. This happens through carrying the virtue of "providing for our own" to the point of excess concern with accumulating the treasures of the earth. I believe this relationship identifies materialism as a peculiar Mormon weakness, a classic example of how Satan can persuade some to drive a legitimate strength to such excess that it becomes a disabling weakness.

19. A desire to follow a prophet is surely a great and appropriate strength, but even this has its potentially dangerous manifestations. I have heard of more than one group whose members are so intent on following the words of a dead prophet that they have rejected the teachings and counsel of the living ones. Satan has used that corruption from the beginning of the Restoration.

You may recall Joseph Smith's direction for the Saints to gather in Kirtland, Ohio, then in Missouri, then in Illinois. At each place along the way, a certain number of Saints fell away, crying "fallen prophet" as their excuse for adhering to the earlier words and rejecting the current direction. The same thing happened after the death of the Prophet Joseph Smith, when some Saints seized upon one statement or another by the deceased Prophet as a basis for sponsoring or joining a new group that rejected the counsel of the living prophets.

Following the prophet is a great strength, but it needs to be consistent and current, lest it lead to the spiritual downfall that comes from rejecting continuous revelation. Under this principle, the most important difference between dead prophets and living ones is that those who are dead are not here to receive and declare the Lord's latest words to His people. If they were, there would be no differences among the messages of the prophets.

A related distortion is seen in the practice of those who select a few sentences from the teachings of a prophet to use in supporting their political agenda or other personal purposes. In doing so, they typically ignore the contrary implications of other prophetic words, or even the clear example of the prophet's own actions. For example, I have corresponded with several Church members who sought to use something President Ezra Taft Benson is quoted as saying as a basis for refusing to file an income tax return or to pay income taxes. I have tried to persuade these persons that their interpretation cannot be what President Benson intended because both he and his predecessors in that sacred office, and all of the General Authorities, have faithfully filed their income tax returns and paid the taxes required by law.

The servants of God are under the Master's commands to follow Him and to be examples to the flock (1 Timothy 4:12; 1 Peter 5:3). We should interpret their words in the light of their walk. To wrest the words of a prophet to support a private agenda, political or financial or otherwise, is to try to *manipulate* the prophet, not to *follow* him.

20. Other strengths that can be used for our downfall are the gifts of love and tolerance. Clearly, these are great virtues. Love is an ultimate quality, and tolerance is its handmaiden. Love and tolerance are pluralistic, and that is their strength, but it is also the source of their potential weakness. Love and tolerance are incomplete unless they are accompanied by a concern for truth and a commitment to the unity God has commanded of His servants.

Carried to an undisciplined excess, love and tolerance can produce indifference to truth and justice and opposition to unity.

What makes mankind "free" from death and sin is not merely love but love accompanied by truth. "And ye shall know the truth, and the truth shall make you free" (John 8:32). And the test of whether we are the Lord's is not just love and tolerance but unity. "If ye are not one," the risen Lord said, "ye are not mine" (D&C 38:27). To follow the Lord's example of love, we must remember His explanation that "whom I love I also chasten" (D&C 95:1), and that He chastens us "that [we] might be one" (D&C 61:8).

At this point, as I draw near to my conclusion, I caution that the very nature of this message could tend to the same downfall that it warns against. The idea that our strengths can become our weaknesses could be understood to imply that we should have "moderation in all things." But the Savior said that if we are luke-warm, He will spew us out of His mouth (Revelation 3:16). Moderation in all things is not a virtue because it would seem to justify moderation in commitment. That is not moderation but indifference. That kind of moderation runs counter to the divine commands to serve with all of our "heart, might, mind and strength" (D&C 4:2), to "seek . . . earnestly the riches of eternity" (D&C 68:31), and to be "valiant in the testimony of Jesus" (D&C 76:79). Moderation is not the answer.

How, then, do we prevent our strengths from becoming our downfall? The quality we must cultivate is humility. Humility is the great protector. Humility is the antidote against pride. Humility is the catalyst for all learning, especially spiritual things.

Through the prophet Ether, the Lord gave us this great insight into the role of humility: "I give unto men weakness that they may be humble; and my grace is sufficient for all men that humble themselves before me; for if they humble themselves before me, and have faith in me, then will I make weak things become strong unto them" (Ether 12:27).

We might also say that if men and women humble themselves before God, He will help them prevent their strengths from becoming weaknesses that the adversary can exploit to destroy them. If we are meek and humble enough to receive counsel, the Lord can and will guide us through the counsel of our parents, our teachers, and our leaders. The proud can only hear the clamor of the crowd, but a person who "becometh as a child," as King Benjamin said, "submissive, meek [and] humble" (Mosiah 3:19), can hear and follow the still small voice by which our Father in Heaven guides His children who are receptive.

Those of us who engage in self-congratulation over a supposed strength have lost the protection of humility and are vulnerable to Satan's using that strength to produce our downfall. In contrast, if we are humble and teachable, hearkening to the commandments of God, the counsel of His leaders, and the promptings of His spirit, we can be guided in how to use our spiritual gifts, accomplishments, and other strengths for righteousness. And we can be guided in how to avoid Satan's efforts to use our strengths to cause our downfall.

In all of this, we should remember and rely on the Lord's direction and promise: "Be thou humble; and the Lord thy God shall lead thee by the hand, and give thee answer to thy prayers" (D&C 112:10).

From an address delivered at Brigham Young University on June 7, 1992, and published in the Ensign, *October 1994, 11–19.*

Notes

1. "Satan—The Great Deceiver," *Ensign,* June 1971, 35, 36.
2. *The Miracle of Forgiveness,* Salt Lake City: Bookcraft, 218–19.
3. "The Only True and Living Church," *Ensign,* December 1971, 41–42.
4. *Doctrinal New Testament Commentary,* 3 vols., Salt Lake City: Bookcraft, 1965–73, 3:361.

17

WEIGHTIER MATTERS

IN DENOUNCING THE SCRIBES and Pharisees, Jesus said, "Ye pay tithe of mint and anise and cummin, and have omitted the *weightier matters* of the law, judgment, mercy, and faith: these ought ye to have done, and not to leave the other undone" (Matthew 23:23; emphasis added).

If we allow ourselves to focus exclusively on lesser matters, we too may overlook the "weightier matters." The weightier matters to which I refer are the qualities like faith and the love of God and His work that will move us strongly toward our eternal goals.

In speaking of weightier matters, I seek to contrast our ultimate goals in eternity with the mortal methods or short-term objectives we use to pursue them. The Apostle Paul wrote, "We look not at the things which are seen, but at the things which are not seen: for the things which are seen are temporal; but the things which are not seen are eternal" (2 Corinthians 4:18).

If we concentrate too intently on our obvious earthly methods or objectives, we can lose sight of our eternal goals, which the apostle called "things . . . not seen." If we do this, we can forget where we should be headed and, in eternal terms, go nowhere. We do not improve our position in eternity just by flying farther and faster in mortality but by moving knowledgeably in the right direction. As the Lord has told us in modern revelation, "That which the Spirit testifies unto you . . . ye should do in all holiness of heart, walking uprightly before me, *considering the end of your salvation*" (D&C 46:7; emphasis added).

We must not confuse means and ends. The vehicle is not the destination. If we lose sight of our eternal goals, we might think the most important thing is how fast we are moving and that any road will get us to our destination. The Apostle Paul described this attitude as "hav[ing] a zeal of God, but not according to knowledge" (Romans 10:2). Zeal is a method, not a goal. Zeal—even a zeal toward God—needs to be "according to knowledge" of God's commandments and His plan for His children. In other words, the weightier matter of the eternal goal must not be displaced by the mortal method, however excellent in itself. I will give three examples.

Family

All Latter-day Saints understand that having an eternal family is an eternal goal. Exaltation is a family matter, not possible outside the everlasting covenant of marriage, which makes possible the perpetuation of glorious family relationships. But this does not mean that everything related to mortal families is an eternal goal. Many short-term objectives associated with families, such as family togetherness and family solidarity, are methods, not the eternal goals we pursue in priority above all others. For example, family solidarity to conduct an evil enterprise is obviously no virtue. Neither is family solidarity to conceal and perpetuate some evil practice like abuse.

The purpose of mortal families is to bring children into the world, to teach them what is right, and to prepare all family members for exaltation in eternal family relationships. The gospel plan contemplates the kind of family government, discipline, solidarity, and love that serve those ultimate goals. But even the love of family members is subject to the overriding first commandment, which is love of God (Matthew 22:37–38). As Jesus taught, "He that loveth father or mother more than me is not worthy of me: and he that loveth son or daughter more than me is not worthy of me" (Matthew 10:37).

Choice or Agency

My next example in this consideration of weightier matters is the role of choice or agency. Few concepts have more potential to mislead us than the idea that choice or agency is an ultimate goal. For Latter-day Saints, this potential confusion is partly a product of the fact that moral agency—the right to choose—is a fundamental condition of mortal life. Without this precious gift of God, the purpose of mortal life could not be realized. To secure our agency in mortality we fought a mighty contest the book of Revelation calls a "war in heaven." This premortal contest ended with the devil and his angels being cast out of heaven and being denied the opportunity of having a body in mortal life (Revelation 12:7–9).

But our war to secure agency was won. The test in this postwar mortal estate is not to secure choice but to use it—to choose good instead of evil so that we can achieve our eternal goals. In mortality, choice is a method, not a goal.

Of course, mortals must still resolve many questions concerning what restrictions or consequences should be placed upon choices. But those questions come under the heading of freedom, not agency. Many do not understand that important fact. For example, when I was serving as president of Brigham Young University, I heard many arguments about the university's honor code or dress and grooming standards that went like this: "It is wrong for BYU to take away my free agency by forcing me to keep certain rules in order to be admitted or permitted to continue as a student." If that silly reasoning were valid, then the Lord, who gave us our agency, took it away when He gave the Ten Commandments. We are responsible to use our agency in a world of choices. It will not do to pretend that our agency has been taken away when we are not free to exercise it without unwelcome consequences.

Because choice is a method, choices can be exercised either way on any matter, and our choices can serve any goal. Therefore, those who consider freedom of choice as a goal can easily slip into the position of trying to justify any choice they make. Choice can even become a slogan to justify one particular choice. For example, one who says "I am pro-choice" is clearly understood as opposing any legal restrictions upon a woman's choice to abort a fetus at any point in her pregnancy.

Almost forty years ago, as a young law professor, I published one of the earliest articles on the legal consequences of abortion. Since that time I have been a knowledgeable observer of the national debate and the unfortunate Supreme Court decisions on the so-called "right to abortion." I have been fascinated with how cleverly those who sought and now defend legalized abortion on demand have moved the issue away from a debate on the moral, ethical, and medical pros and cons of legal restrictions on abortion and focused the debate on the slogan or issue of choice. The slogan or sound bite "pro-choice" has had an almost magical effect in justifying abortion and in neutralizing opposition to it.

Pro-choice slogans have been particularly seductive to Latter-day Saints because we know that moral agency, which can be described as the power of choice, is a fundamental necessity in the gospel plan. All Latter-day Saints are pro-choice according to that theological definition. But being pro-choice on the need for moral agency does not end the matter for us. Choice is a method, not the ultimate goal. We are accountable for our choices, and only righteous choices will move us toward our eternal goals.

In this effort, Latter-day Saints follow the teachings of the prophets. On this subject our prophetic guidance is clear. The Lord commanded, "Thou shalt not . . . kill, nor do anything like unto it" (D&C 59:6). The Church opposes elective abortion for personal or social convenience. Our members are taught that, subject only to some very rare exceptions, they must not submit to, perform, encourage, pay for, or arrange for an abortion. That direction tells us what we need to do on the weightier matters of the law, the choices that will move us toward eternal life.

In today's world we are not true to our teachings if we are merely pro-choice. We must stand up for the *right* choice. Those who persist in refusing to think beyond slogans and sound bites like "pro-choice" wander from the goals they pretend to espouse and wind up giving their support to results they might not support if those results were presented without disguise.

For example, consider the uses some have made of the possible exceptions to our firm teachings against abortion. Our leaders have taught that the only possible exceptions are when the pregnancy results from rape or incest, when a competent physician has determined that the life or health of the mother is in serious jeopardy, or when the fetus has severe defects that will not allow the baby to survive beyond birth. But even these exceptions do not justify abortion automatically. Because abortion is a most serious matter, we are counseled that it should be considered only after the persons responsible have consulted with their bishops and received divine confirmation through prayer.

Some Latter-day Saints say they deplore abortion, but they give these exceptional circumstances as a basis for their pro-choice position that the law should allow abortion on demand in all circumstances. Such persons should face the reality that the circumstances described in these three exceptions are extremely rare. For example, conception by incest or rape—the circumstance most commonly cited by those who use exceptions to argue for abortion on demand—are involved in only a tiny minority of abortions. More than 95 percent of the millions of abortions performed each year extinguish the life of a fetus conceived by consensual relations. Thus, the effect in more than 95 percent of abortions is not to vindicate choice but to avoid its consequences.[1] Using arguments of "choice" to try to justify altering the consequences of choice is a classic case of omitting what the Savior called "the weightier matters of the law."

A prominent basis for the secular or philosophical arguments for abortion on demand is the argument that a woman should have control over her own body. A letter I received from a thoughtful Latter-day Saint outside the United States analyzed that argument in secular terms. Since his analysis reaches the same conclusion I have urged on religious grounds, I quote it here for the benefit of those most subject to persuasion on this basis:

"Every woman has, within the limits of nature, the right to choose what will or will not happen to her body. Every woman has, at the same time, the responsibility for the way she uses her body. If by her choice she behaves in such a way that a human fetus is conceived, she has not only the right to but also the responsibility for that fetus. If it is an unwanted pregnancy, she is not justified in ending it with the claim that it interferes with her right to choose. She herself chose what would happen to her body by risking pregnancy. She had her choice. If she has no better reason, her conscience should tell her that abortion would be a highly irresponsible choice.

"What constitutes a good reason? Since a human fetus has intrinsic and infinite human value, the only good reason for an abortion would be the violation or deprivation of, or the threat to, the woman's right to choose what will or will not happen to her body. Social, educational, financial, and personal considerations alone do not outweigh the value of the life that is in the fetus. These considerations by themselves may properly lead to the decision to place the baby for adoption after its birth but not to end its existence in utero.

"The woman's right to choose what will or will not happen to her body is obviously violated by rape or incest. When conception results in such a case, the woman has the moral as well as the legal right to an abortion because the condition of pregnancy is the result of someone else's irresponsibility, not hers. She does not have to take responsibility for it. To force her by law to carry the fetus to term would be a further violation of her right. She also has the right to refuse an abortion. This would give her the right to the fetus and also the responsibility for it. She could later relinquish this right and this responsibility through the process of placing the baby for adoption after it is born. Whichever way is a responsible choice."[2]

The man who wrote those words also applied the same reasoning to the other exceptions allowed by our doctrine—the life or health of the mother, and a baby that will not survive beyond birth.

I conclude this discussion of choice with two more short points. If we say we are antiabortion in our personal life but prochoice in public policy, we are saying that we will not use our influence to establish public policies that encourage righteous choices on matters God's servants have defined as serious sins. I urge Latter-day Saints who have taken that position to ask themselves which other grievous sins should be decriminalized or smiled on by the law on this theory that persons should not be hampered in their choices. Should we decriminalize or lighten the legal consequences of child abuse? Of cruelty to animals? Of fraud? Of fathers who choose to abandon their families for greater freedom or convenience? Of pollution?

Similarly, some reach the pro-choice position by saying we should not legislate morality. Those who take this position should realize that the law of crimes legislates nothing but morality. Should we repeal all laws with a moral basis so our government will not punish any choices some persons consider immoral? Such an action would wipe out virtually all laws against crimes.

Diversity

My third illustration of the bad effects of confusing means and ends, methods and goals, concerns the word *diversity*. Not many labels have produced more confused thinking in our time than this one. A respected federal judge recently commented on current changes in culture and values by observing that "a new credo in celebration of diversity seems to be emerging which proclaims, 'Divided We Stand!' "[3] Even in religious terms, we sometimes hear "celebrations of diversity," as if diversity were an ultimate goal.

The word *diversity* has legitimate uses to describe a condition. Thus, wherever differences among the children of God are described in the scriptures, such as in the numerous scriptural references to nations, kindreds, tongues, and peoples, we have a description of a condition of diversity.

In the scriptures, the objectives we are taught to pursue on the way to our eternal goals are ideals like love and obedience. These ideals do not accept us as we are but require each of us to make changes. Jesus did not pray that His followers would be "diverse." He prayed that they would be "one" (John 17:21–22). Modern revelation does not say, "Be diverse; and if ye are not diverse, ye are not mine." It says, "Be one; and if ye are not one ye are not mine" (D&C 38:27).

Since diversity is a condition, a method, or a short-term objective—not an ultimate goal—whenever diversity is urged it is appropriate to ask, "What kind of diversity?" or "Diversity in what circumstance or condition?" or "Diversity in furtherance of what goal?" This is especially important in our policy debates, which should be conducted not in terms of slogans but in terms of the goals we seek and the methods or shorter-term objectives that will achieve them. Diversity for its own sake is meaningless and can clearly be shown to lead to unacceptable results. For example, if diversity is the underlying goal for a neighborhood, does this mean we should take affirmative action to assure that the neighborhood include thieves and pedophiles, slaughterhouses and water hazards? Diversity can be a good method to achieve some long-term goal, but public policy discussions need to get beyond the slogan to identify the goal, to specify the proposed diversity, and to explain how this kind of diversity will help to achieve the goal.

Our Church has an approach to the obvious cultural and ethnic diversities among our members. We teach that what unites us is far more important than what divides us. Consequently, our members are asked to concentrate their efforts to strengthen our unity—not to glorify our diversity. For example, our objective is not to organize local wards and branches according to differences in culture, ethnic, or national origins, although that effect is sometimes produced on a temporary basis when required because of language barriers. Instead, we teach that members of majority groupings (whatever their nature) are responsible to accept Church members of other groupings, providing full fellowship and full opportunities in Church participation. We seek to establish a community of Saints—"one body," the Apostle Paul called it (1 Corinthians 12:13)—where everyone feels needed and wanted, and where all can pursue the eternal goals we share.

Consistent with the Savior's command to "be one," we seek unity. On this subject President Gordon B. Hinckley has taught:

"I remember when President J. Reuben Clark, Jr., as a counselor in the First Presidency, would stand at this pulpit and plead for unity among the priesthood. I think he was not asking that we give up our individual personalities and become as robots cast from a single mold. I am confident he was not asking that we cease to think, to meditate, to ponder as individuals. I think he was telling us that if we are to assist in moving forward the work of God, we must carry in our hearts a united conviction concerning the great basic foundation stones of our faith. . . . If we are to assist in moving forward the work of God, we must carry in our hearts a united conviction that the ordinances and covenants of this work are eternal and everlasting in their consequences."[4]

Anyone who preaches unity risks misunderstanding. The same is true of anyone who questions the goal of diversity. Such a one risks being thought intolerant. But tolerance is not jeopardized by promoting unity or by challenging diversity. President Hinckley also said:

"Each of us is an individual. Each of us is different. There must be respect for those differences. . . . We must work harder to build mutual respect, an attitude of forbearance, with tolerance one for another regardless of the doctrines and philosophies which we may espouse. Concerning these you and I may disagree. But we can do so with respect and civility. . . .

"An article of the faith to which I subscribe states: 'We claim the privilege of worshipping Almighty God according to the dictates of our own conscience, and allow all men the same privilege, let them worship how, where, or what they may' (Article of Faith 11). I hope to find myself always on the side of those defending this position. Our strength lies in our freedom to choose. There is strength even in our very diversity. But there is greater strength in the God-given mandate to each of us to work for the uplift and blessing of all His sons and daughters, regardless of their ethnic or national origin or other differences."[5]

In short, we preach unity among the community of Saints and tolerance toward the personal differences that are inevitable in the beliefs and conduct of a diverse population. Tolerance obviously requires a noncontentious manner of relating toward one another's differences. But tolerance does not require abandoning one's standards or opinions on political or public policy choices. Tolerance is a way of reacting to diversity, not a command to insulate it from examination.

Strong calls for diversity in the public sector sometimes have the effect of pressuring those holding majority opinions to abandon fundamental values to accommodate the diverse positions of those in the minority. Usually this does not substitute a minority value for a majority one. Rather, it seeks to achieve "diversity" by abandoning the official value position altogether, so that no one's value will be contradicted by an official or semiofficial position. The result of this abandonment is not a diversity of values but an official anarchy of values. I believe this is an example of what an astute observer has characterized as using diversity "as a euphemism for moral relativism."[6]

There are many examples of the pressure for diversity resulting in the anarchy of values we call moral relativism. These examples include such varied proposals as forbidding the public schools to teach the wrongfulness of certain behavior or the rightfulness of patriotism and attempting to banish a representation of the Ten Commandments from any public buildings.

In a day when prominent thinkers like James Billington and Allan Bloom have decried the fact that our universities have stopped teaching right and wrong, we are grateful for the countercultural position we enjoy at Brigham Young University and in our seminaries and institutes of religion.

In conclusion, diversity and choice are not the weightier matters of the law. The weightier matters that move us toward our goals of eternal life are love of God, obedience to His commandments, and unity in accomplishing the work of His Church. In this belief and practice we move against the powerful modern tides running toward individualism and tolerance rather than toward obedience and cooperative action. Though our belief and practice is unpopular, it is right, and it does not require the blind obedience or the stifling uniformity its critics charge. If we are united on our eternal goal and united on the inspired principles that will get us there, we can be diverse on individual efforts that support our goals and that are consistent with those principles.

We know that the work of God cannot be done without unity and cooperative action. We also know that the children of God cannot be exalted as single individuals. Neither a man nor a woman can be exalted in the celestial kingdom unless both unite in the unselfishness of the everlasting covenant of marriage and unless both choose to keep the commandments and honor the covenants of that united state.

As the one whose atonement paid the incomprehensible price for our sins, Jesus Christ is the one who can prescribe the conditions for our salvation. He has commanded us to keep His commandments (John 14:15) and to "be one" (D&C 38:27). I pray that we will make the wise choices to keep the commandments and to seek the unity that will move us toward our ultimate goal, "eternal life, which gift is the greatest of all the gifts of God" (D&C 14:7).

From an address delivered at Brigham Young University on February 9, 1999, and published in the Ensign, *January 2001, 12–17.*

NOTES

1. Russell M. Nelson, "Reverence for Life," *Ensign,* May 1985, 11–14.
2. Letter to the author, 20 January 1999.
3. J. Thomas Greene, "Activist Judicial Philosophies on Trial," *Federal Rules Decisions* 178, 1997: 200.
4. *Teachings of Gordon B. Hinckley,* Salt Lake City: Deseret Book, 1997, 672.
5. *Teachings of Gordon B. Hinckley,* 661, 665, 664.
6. BYU visiting professor Louis Pojman, "Opinion," *Universe,* 13 October 1998, 4.

18

JUDGE NOT AND JUDGING

A S A STUDENT OF THE SCRIPTURES and as a former judge, I have had a special interest in the many scriptures that refer to judging. The best known of these is "Judge not, that ye be not judged" (3 Nephi 14:1; Matthew 7:1).

I have been puzzled that some scriptures command us *not* to judge, while other scriptures instruct us that we *should* judge and even tell us how to do it. But as I have studied these scriptural passages I have become convinced that these seemingly contradictory directions are consistent when we view them with the perspective of eternity. The key is to understand that there are two kinds of judging: final judgments, which we are forbidden to make, and intermediate judgments, which we are directed to make, but upon righteous principles. I will discuss gospel judging.

Final Judgments

Final judgment is that future occasion in which all of us will stand before the judgment seat of Christ to be judged according to our works (1 Nephi 15:33; 3 Nephi 27:15; Mormon 3:20; D&C 19:3). Some Christians look on this as the time when individuals are assigned to heaven or hell. With the increased understanding we have received from the Restoration, Latter-day Saints understand the final judgment as the time when all mankind will receive their personal "dominion in the mansions which are prepared" for them in the various kingdoms of glory (D&C 76:111; John 14:2; 1 Corinthians 15:40–44). I believe that the scriptural command to "judge not" refers most clearly to this final judgment, as in the Book of Mormon declaration that "man shall not . . . judge; for judgment is mine, saith the Lord" (Mormon 8:20).

Since mortals cannot suppose that they will be acting as final judges at that future, sacred time, why did the Savior command that we not judge final judgments? I believe this commandment was given because we presume to make final judgments whenever we proclaim that any particular person is going to hell (or to heaven) for a particular act or at a particular time. When we do this—and there is great temptation to do so—we hurt ourselves and the person we pretend to judge.

The effect of our attempting to pass final judgment on another is analogous to the effect on an athlete and on the observers of an athletic contest if we could proclaim the outcome of the contest with certainty while it was still under way. A similar reason forbids our presuming to make final judgments on the outcome of any person's lifelong mortal contest.

The Prophet Joseph Smith said: "While one portion of the human race is judging and condemning the other without mercy, the Great Parent of the universe looks upon the whole of the human family with a fatherly care and paternal regard; . . . He holds the reins of judgment in His hands; He is a wise Lawgiver, and will judge all men, . . . 'Not according to what they have not, but according to what they have,' those who have lived without law, will be judged without law, and those who have a law, will be judged by that law."[1]

We must refrain from making final judgments on people because we lack the knowledge and the wisdom to do so. We would even apply the wrong standards. The world's way is to judge competitively between winners and losers. The Lord's way of final judgment will be to apply His perfect knowledge of the law a person has received and to judge on the basis of that person's circumstances, motives, and actions throughout his or her entire life (Luke 12:47–48; John 15:22; 2 Nephi 9:25).

Even the Savior, during His mortal ministry, refrained from making final judgments. We see this in the account of the woman taken in adultery. After the crowd who intended to stone her had departed, Jesus asked her about her accusers. "Hath no man condemned thee?" When she answered no, Jesus declared, "Neither do I condemn thee: go, and sin no more" (John 8:10, 11). In this context the word *condemn* apparently refers to the final judgment (John 3:17). The Lord obviously did not justify the woman's sin. He simply told her that He did not condemn her—that is, He would not pass final judgment on her at that time. This interpretation is confirmed by what He then said to the Pharisees: "Ye judge after the flesh; I judge no man" (John 8:15). The woman taken in adultery was granted time to repent, time that would have been denied by those who wanted to stone her.

The Savior gave this same teaching on another occasion: "And if any man hear my words, and believe not, I judge him not: for I came not to judge the world, but to save the world" (John 12:47).

From all of this we see that the final judgment is the Lord's and that mortals must refrain from judging others in the final sense of concluding or proclaiming that they are irretrievably bound for hell or have lost all hope of exaltation.

Intermediate Judgments

In contrast to *forbidding* mortals to make final judgments, the scriptures *require* mortals to make what I will call "intermediate judgments." These judgments are essential to the exercise of personal moral agency. Our scriptural accounts of the Savior's mortal life provide the pattern. He declared, "I have many things to say and to judge of you" (John 8:26), and "For judgment I am come into this world, that they which see not might see" (John 9:39).

During His mortal ministry the Savior made and acted upon many intermediate judgments, such as when He told the Samaritan woman of her sinful life (John 4:17–19), when He rebuked the scribes and Pharisees for their hypocrisy (see Matthew 15:1–9; 23:1–33), and when He commented on the comparative merit of the offerings of the rich men and of the widow's mites (Mark 12:41–44).

Church leaders are specifically commanded to judge. Thus, the Lord said to Alma, "Whosoever transgresseth against men, him shall ye judge according to the sins which he has committed; and if he confess his sins before thee and me, and repenteth in the sincerity of his heart, him shall ye forgive, and I will forgive him also. . . . And whosoever will not repent of his sins the same shall not be numbered among my people" (Mosiah 26:29, 32). Similarly, in modern revelation the Lord appointed the bishop to be a "judge in Israel" to judge over property and transgressions (D&C 58:17; 107:72).

The Savior also commanded individuals to be judges, both of circumstances and of other people. Through the prophet Moses, the Lord commanded Israel, "Ye shall do no unrighteousness in judgment: thou shalt not respect the person of the poor, nor honour the person of the mighty: but in righteousness shalt thou judge thy neighbour" (Leviticus 19:15).

On one occasion the Savior chided the people, "Why even of yourselves judge ye not what is right?" (Luke 12:57). On another occasion He said, "Judge not according to the appearance, but judge righteous judgment" (John 7:24).

We must, of course, make judgments every day in the exercise of our moral agency, but we must be careful that our judgments of people are intermediate and not final. Thus, our Savior's teachings contain many commandments we cannot keep without making intermediate judgments of people: "Give not that which is holy unto the dogs, neither cast ye your pearls before swine" (Matthew 7:6); "Beware of false prophets. . . . Ye shall know them by their fruits" (Matthew 7:15–16); and "Go ye out from among the wicked" (D&C 38:42).

We all make judgments in choosing our friends, in choosing how we will spend our time and our money, and, of course, in choosing an eternal companion. Some of these intermediate judgments are surely among those the Savior referenced when he taught that "the weightier matters of the law" include judgment (Matthew 23:23).

Righteous Intermediate Judgment

The scriptures not only command or contemplate that we will make intermediate judgments but also give us some guidance—some governing principles—on how to do so.

The most fundamental principle is contained in the Savior's commandment that we "judge not unrighteously, . . . but judge righteous judgment" (JST, Matthew 7:1–2, footnote a; John 7:24; Alma 41:14). Let us consider some principles or ingredients that lead to a "righteous judgment."

First, a righteous judgment must, by definition, be intermediate. It will refrain from declaring that a person has been assured of exaltation or from dismissing a person as being irrevocably bound for hell. It will refrain from declaring that a person has forfeited all opportunity for exaltation or even all opportunity for a useful role in the work of the Lord. The gospel is a gospel of hope, and none of us is authorized to deny the power of the Atonement to bring about a cleansing of individual sins and forgiveness, and a reformation of life on appropriate conditions.

Second, a righteous judgment will be guided by the Spirit of the Lord, not by anger, revenge, jealousy, or self-interest. The Book of Mormon teaches, "For behold, my brethren, it is given unto you to judge, that ye may know good from evil; and the way to judge is as plain . . . as the daylight is from the dark night. For behold, the Spirit of Christ is given to every man, that he may know good from evil" (Moroni 7:15–16).

The Savior taught that one of the missions of the Comforter He would send would be to assist in the judgment of the world by guiding the faithful "into all truth" (John 16:13; 16: 8, 11).

Third, to be righteous, an intermediate judgment must be within our stewardship. We should not presume to exercise and act upon judgments that are outside our personal responsibilities. Some time ago I attended an adult Sunday School class in a small town in Utah. The subject was the sacrament, and the class was being taught by the bishop. During class discussion a member asked, "What if you see an unworthy person partaking of the sacrament? What do you do?" The bishop answered, "You do nothing. I may need to do something." That wise answer illustrates my point about stewardship in judging.

Fourth, we should, if possible, refrain from judging until we have adequate knowledge of the facts. In an essay titled "Sitting in the Seat of Judgment," the great essayist William George Jordan reminded us that character cannot be judged as dress goods—by viewing a sample yard to represent a whole bolt of cloth.[2]

In another essay Jordan wrote: "There is but one quality necessary for the perfect understanding of character, one quality that, if man have it, he may *dare to judge*—that is, omniscience. Most people study character as a proofreader pores over a great poem: his ears are dulled to the majesty and music of the lines, his eyes are darkened to the magic imagination of the genius of the author; that proofreader is busy watching for an inverted comma, a misspacing, or a wrong font letter. He has an eye trained for the imperfections, the weaknesses. . . .

"We do not need to judge nearly so much as we think we do. This is the age of snap judgments. . . . [We need] the courage to say, 'I don't know. I am waiting further evidence. I must hear both sides of the question.' It is this suspended judgment that is the supreme form of charity."[3]

Someone has said that you cannot slice cheese so fine that it doesn't have two sides.

Two experiences illustrate the importance of caution in judging. A Relief Society worker visiting a sister in her ward asked whether the woman's married children ever visited her. Because of a short-term memory loss, this elderly sister innocently answered no. So informed, her visitor and others spoke criticisms of her children for neglecting their mother. In fact, one of her children visited her at least daily, and all of them helped her in many ways. They were innocent of neglect and should not have been judged on the basis of an inadequate knowledge of the facts.

Another such circumstance was described in an *Ensign* article by Brigham Young University professor Arthur R. Bassett. He stated that while teaching an institute class, "I was troubled when one person whispered to another all through the opening prayer. The guilty parties were not hard to spot because they continued whispering all through the class. I kept glaring at them, hoping that they would take the hint, but they didn't seem to notice. Several times during the hour, I was tempted to ask them to take their conversation outside if they felt it was so urgent—but fortunately something kept me from giving vent to my feelings.

"After the class, one of them came to me and apologized that she hadn't explained to me before class that her friend was deaf. The friend could read lips, but since I was discussing—as I often do—with my back to the class, writing at the chalkboard and talking over my shoulder, my student had been 'translating' for her friend, telling her what I was saying. To this day I am thankful that both of us were spared the embarrassment that might have occurred had I given vent to a judgment made without knowing the facts."[4]

The scriptures give a specific caution against judging when we cannot know all the facts. King Benjamin taught:

"Perhaps thou shalt say: The man has brought upon himself his misery; therefore I will stay my hand, and will not give unto him of my food, nor impart unto him of my substance that he may not suffer, for his punishments are just—

"But I say unto you, O man, whosoever doeth this the same hath great cause to repent; and except he repenteth of that which he hath done he perisheth forever, and hath no interest in the kingdom of God. . . .

"And if ye judge the man who putteth up his petition to you for your substance that he perish not, and condemn him, how much more just will be your condemnation for withholding your substance" (Mosiah 4:17–18, 22).

There is one qualification to this principle that we should not judge people without an adequate knowledge of the facts. Sometimes urgent circumstances require us to make preliminary judgments before we can get all the facts we desire for our decision making.

From time to time some diligent defenders deny this reality, such as the writer of a letter to the editor who insisted that certain publicly reported conduct should be ignored because "in this country you are innocent until you are proven guilty." The presumption of innocence until proven guilty in a court of law is a vital rule to guide the conduct of a criminal trial, but it is not a valid restraint on personal decisions. There are important restraints upon our intermediate judgments, but the presumption of innocence is not one of them.

Some personal decisions must be made before we have access

to all the facts. Two hypotheticals illustrate this principle: (1) If a particular person has been arrested for child sexual abuse and is free on bail awaiting trial on his guilt or innocence, would you trust him to tend your children while you take a weekend trip? (2) If a person you have trusted with your property has been indicted for embezzlement, would you continue to leave him in charge of your life savings? In such circumstances we do the best we can, relying ultimately on the teaching in modern scripture that we should put our "trust in that Spirit which leadeth to do good—yea, to do justly, to walk humbly, to judge righteously" (D&C 11:12).

A fifth principle of a righteous intermediate judgment is that whenever possible we will refrain from judging people and only judge situations. This is essential whenever we attempt to act upon different standards than others with whom we must associate—at home, at work, or in the community. We can set and act upon high standards for ourselves or our homes without condemning those who do otherwise.

For example, I know of an LDS family with an older teenage son who has become addicted to smoking. The parents have insisted that he not smoke in their home or in front of his younger siblings. That is a wise judgment of a situation, not a person. Then, even as the parents take protective measures pertaining to a regrettable situation, they need to maintain loving relations and encourage improved conduct by the precious person.

In an *Ensign* article, an anonymous victim of childhood sexual abuse illustrates the contrast between judging situations and judging persons. The article begins with heart-wrenching words and with true statements of eternal principles:

"I am a survivor of childhood physical, emotional, and sexual abuse. I no longer view myself as a victim. The change has come from inside me—my attitude. I do not need to destroy myself with anger and hate. I don't need to entertain thoughts of revenge. My Savior knows what happened. He knows the truth.

He can make the judgments and the punishments. He will be just. I will leave it in His hands. I will not be judged for what happened to me, but I will be judged by how I let it affect my life. I am responsible for my actions and what I do with my knowledge. I am not to blame for what happened to me as a child. I cannot change the past. But I can change the future. I have chosen to heal myself and pass on to my children what I have learned. The ripples in my pond will spread through future generations."[5]

Sixth, forgiveness is a companion principle to the commandment that in final judgments we judge not and in intermediate judgments we judge righteously. The Savior taught, "Judge not, and ye shall not be judged: condemn not, and ye shall not be condemned: forgive, and ye shall be forgiven" (Luke 6:37). In modern revelation the Lord has declared, "I, the Lord, will forgive whom I will forgive, but of you it is required to forgive all men" (D&C 64:10).

Pursuing that principle, the author of the *Ensign* article writes: "Somewhere along the journey of healing comes the essential task of forgiving. Often the command to forgive (see D&C 64:10) seems almost more than one can bear, but this eternal principle can bring lasting peace."

This article also quotes another survivor of abuse: "I love that truth that although I need to evaluate situations, . . . I do not need to condemn or judge my abusers nor be part of the punishment. I leave all that to the Lord. I used the principle of forgiveness to strengthen me."[6]

Seventh, a final ingredient or principle of a righteous judgment is that it will apply righteous standards. If we apply unrighteous standards, our judgment will be unrighteous. By falling short of righteous standards, we place ourselves in jeopardy of being judged by incorrect or unrighteous standards ourselves. The fundamental scripture on the whole subject of not judging contains this warning: "For with what judgment ye judge, ye shall be judged: and with what measure ye mete, it shall be measured to you again" (Matthew 7:2; 3 Nephi 14:2).

The prophet Mormon taught, "Seeing that ye know the light by which ye may judge, which light is the light of Christ, see that ye do not judge wrongfully; for with that same judgment which ye judge ye shall also be judged" (Moroni 7:18).

A judgment can be unrighteous because its standards are too harsh—the consequences are too severe for the gravity of the wrong and the needs of the wrongdoer. I remember a conversation with an LDS newspaperwoman who described what happened when she reported that the Prophet Joseph Smith received the golden plates in 1826, a mistake of one year from the actual date of 1827. She said she received about ten phone calls from outraged Latter-day Saints who would not accept her admission of error and sincere apology and even berated her with abusive language. I wonder if persons who cannot handle an honest mistake without abusing the individual can stand up to having their own mistakes judged by so severe a standard.

In a Brigham Young University devotional address, Professor Catherine Corman Parry gave a memorable scriptural illustration of the consequences of judging by the wrong standards. The scripture is familiar. Martha received Jesus into her house and worked to provide for Him while her sister, Mary, sat at Jesus' feet and heard His words.

"But Martha was cumbered about much serving, and came to him, and said, Lord, dost thou not care that my sister hath left me to serve alone? Bid her therefore that she help me.

"And Jesus answered and said unto her, Martha, Martha, thou art careful and troubled about many things: But one thing is needful: and Mary hath chosen that good part, which shall not be taken away from her" (Luke 10:40–42).

Professor Parry said: "The Lord acknowledges Martha's care: 'Martha, Martha, thou art careful and troubled about many things' (v. 41). Then he delivers the gentle but clear rebuke. But the rebuke would not have come had Martha not prompted it. The Lord did not go into the kitchen and tell Martha to stop cooking and come listen. Apparently he was content to let her serve him however she cared to, until she judged another person's service: 'Lord, dost thou not care that my sister hath left me to serve alone? Bid her therefore that she help me' (v. 40). Martha's self-importance, expressed through her judgment of her sister, occasioned the Lord's rebuke, not her busyness with the meal."[7]

In subsequent portions of her talk, Professor Parry observed that in this instance—and also in the example of Simon the Pharisee, who criticized the woman who anointed the feet of the Savior (Luke 7:36–50)—Jesus took one individual's judgment of another individual as a standard and applied that judgment to the individual who was judging. "Quite literally they were measured by their own standards and found wanting," she observed.

" . . . While there are many things we must make judgments about, the sins of another or the state of our own souls in comparison to others seems not to be among them. . . . Our own sins, no matter how few or seemingly insignificant, disqualify us as judges of other people's sins."[8]

I love the words in Susan Evans McCloud's familiar hymn:

> Who am I to judge another
> When I walk imperfectly?
> In the quiet heart is hidden
> Sorrow that the eye can't see.
> Who am I to judge another?
> Lord, I would follow thee.[9]

In one of the monthly General Authority fast and testimony meetings, I heard President James E. Faust say, "The older I get, the less judgmental I become." That wise observation gives us a standard to live by in the matter of judgments. We should refrain from anything that seems to be a final judgment of any person, manifesting our determination to leave final judgments to the Lord, who alone has the capacity to judge.

In the intermediate judgments we must make, we should take care to judge righteously. We should seek the guidance of the Spirit in our decisions. We should limit our judgments to our own stewardships. Whenever possible we should refrain from judging people until we have an adequate knowledge of the facts. So far as possible, we should judge circumstances rather than people. In all our judgments we should apply righteous standards. And in all of this we must remember the command to forgive.

A doctrine underlies the subject of gospel judging. It was taught when a lawyer asked the Savior, "Which is the great commandment in the law?" Jesus answered: "Thou shalt love the Lord thy God with all thy heart, and with all thy soul, and with all thy mind. This is the first and great commandment. And the second is like unto it, Thou shalt love thy neighbour as thyself. On these two commandments hang all the law and the prophets" (Matthew 22:36–40).

Later, in the sublime teachings the Savior gave His apostles on the eve of His suffering and atonement, He said, "A new commandment I give unto you, That ye love one another; as I have loved you, that ye also love one another. By this shall all men know that ye are my disciples, if ye have love one to another" (John 13:34–35).

May God bless us that we may have that love and that we may show it by refraining from making final judgments of our fellowman. In those intermediate judgments we are responsible to make, may we judge righteously and with love. The gospel of Jesus Christ is a gospel of love. Our Master whom we seek to serve is, as the scriptures say, a "God of love" (2 Corinthians 13:11). May we be examples of His love and His gospel.

From an address delivered at Brigham Young University on March 1, 1998, and published in the Ensign, *August 1999, 6–13.*

NOTES

1. *Teachings of the Prophet Joseph Smith,* sel. Joseph Fielding Smith, Salt Lake City: Deseret Book, 1976, 218.
2. *The Crown of Individuality,* New York: F. H. Revell, 1909, 101–5.
3. "The Supreme Charity of the World," in *The Kingship of Self-Control,* New York: F. H. Revell, 1905, 27–30.
4. "Floods, Winds, and the Gates of Hell," *Ensign,* June 1991, 8.
5. "The Journey to Healing," *Ensign,* September 1997, 19.
6. "The Journey to Healing," 22.
7. "'Simon, I Have Somewhat to Say unto Thee': Judgment and Condemnation in the Parables of Jesus," in *Brigham Young University 1990–91 Devotional and Fireside Speeches* 1991, 116.
8. "'Simon, I Have Somewhat to Say unto Thee,'" 116, 118–19.
9. "Lord, I Would Follow Thee," *Hymns of The Church of Jesus Christ of Latter-day Saints,* Salt Lake City: The Church of Jesus Christ of Latter-day Saints, 1985, no. 220.

19

TIMING

THE MOST SIGNIFICANT ACADEMIC talks I heard during my
service at Brigham Young University had one common characteristic. Instead of providing new facts or advocating a particular position, as many lectures do, the most significant talks
changed the listeners' way of thinking about an important subject. Similarly, in this chapter I will attempt to change some read-
ers' ways of thinking about an important subject—the matter of
timing.

I begin with a story I heard many years ago at the inauguration
of a university president. It illustrates the importance of timing in
university administration. One university president had come to
the end of his period of service, and another was just beginning. As
a gesture of goodwill, the wise outgoing president handed his young
successor three sealed envelopes. "Hold these until you have the first
crisis in your administration," he explained. "Then open the first
one, and you will find some valuable advice."

It was a year before the new president had a crisis. When he opened the first envelope, he found a single sheet of paper on which were written the words, "Blame the prior administration." He followed that advice and survived the crisis.

Two years later he faced another serious challenge to his leadership. He opened the second envelope and read, "Reorganize your administration." He did so, and the reorganization disarmed his critics and gave new impetus to his leadership.

Much later the now-seasoned president encountered his third major crisis. Eagerly he opened the last envelope, anticipating the advice that would provide the solution for his troubles. Again he found a single sheet of paper, but this time it read, "Prepare three envelopes." It was time for new leadership.

The familiar observation that "timing is everything" surely overstates the point, but timing *is* vital. We read in Ecclesiastes:

"To every thing there is a season, and a time to every purpose under the heaven: A time to be born, and a time to die; a time to plant, and a time to pluck up that which is planted; . . .

"A time to weep, and a time to laugh; a time to mourn, and a time to dance; . . . [A] time to embrace, and a time to refrain from embracing; . . . [A] time to keep silence, and a time to speak" (Ecclesiastes 3:1–2, 4–5, 7).

In all the important decisions in our lives, what is most important is to *do the right thing*. Of almost equal importance is to *do the right thing at the right time*. People who do the right thing at the wrong time can be frustrated and ineffective. They can even be confused about whether they made the right choice when what was wrong was not their choice but their timing.

The Lord's Timing

My first point on the subject of timing is that the Lord has His own timetable. "My words are sure and shall not fail," the Lord taught the early elders of this dispensation. "But," He continued, "all things must come to pass in their time" (D&C 64:31–32).

The first principle of the gospel is faith in the Lord Jesus Christ. Faith means trust—trust in God's will, trust in His way of doing things, and trust in His timetable. We should not try to impose our timetable on Him. As Elder Neal A. Maxwell has said:

"The issue for us is trusting God enough to trust also His timing. If we can truly believe He has our welfare at heart, may we not let His plans unfold as He thinks best? The same is true with the second coming and with all those matters wherein our faith needs to include faith in the Lord's timing for us personally, not just in His overall plans and purposes."[1]

Elder Maxwell later added, "Since faith in the timing of the Lord may be tried, let us learn to say not only, 'Thy will be done,' but patiently also, 'Thy timing be done.'"[2] Indeed, we cannot have true faith in the Lord without also having complete trust in His will and in His timing.

Among the persons who violate this principle are those who advocate euthanasia. They are trying to take an essential matter that we understand to be determined only by God and accelerate its occurrence according to their own will or preference. In our service in the Lord's church we should remember that *when* is just as important as *who, what, where,* and *how.*

For a vivid illustration of the importance of timing we can look to the earthly ministry of the Lord and His succeeding instructions to His apostles. During His lifetime the Lord instructed the Twelve not to preach to the Gentiles but "rather to the lost sheep of the house of Israel" (Matthew 10:5–6; 15:22–26). Then, at the appropriate time, this instruction was reversed in a great revelation to the Apostle Peter. Only then, at the precise time dictated by the Lord, was the gospel taken to the Gentiles (Acts 10–11).

As this example shows, continuing revelation is the means by which the Lord administers His timing. We need that revelatory direction. For example, many of us or our descendants will doubt-less participate in the fulfillment of prophecies about the build-ing of the city of New Jerusalem (D&C 84:2–4). But in this mat-ter the timing is the Lord's, not ours. We will not be approved or blessed in clearing the ground or pouring the footings for that great project until the Lord has said it is time. In this, as in so many other things, the Lord will proceed in His own time and in His own way.

We prepare in the way the Lord has directed. We hold our-selves in readiness to act on the Lord's timing. He will tell us when the time is right to take the next step. For now, we simply concentrate on our own assignments and on what we have been asked to do today. In this we are also mindful of the Lord's assur-ance: "I will hasten my work in its time" (D&C 88:73).

People who do not accept continuing revelation sometimes get into trouble by doing things too soon or too late or too long. The practice of plural marriage is an example.

The importance of the Lord's timing is also evident in His dietary laws. The Lord gave one dietary direction to ancient Israel. Much later, because of the "evils and designs" that exist in these "last days" (D&C 89:4), He gave us a Word of Wisdom suited to the circumstances of our time, accompanied by the promised blessings we need in our time.

The Lord's timing also applies to the important events of our personal lives. A great scripture in the Doctrine and Covenants declares that a particular spiritual experience will come to us "in his own time, and in his own way, and according to his own will" (D&C 88:68). This principle applies to revelation and to all of the most important events in our lives: birth, marriage, death, and even our moves from place to place.

An example comes from the life of prominent pioneer Anson Call, who was in the initial exodus from Nauvoo. He and his fam-ily crossed Iowa in the spring of 1846 and reached Council Bluffs, Iowa, that summer. There, Brigham Young was organizing wagon companies. He appointed Anson Call captain of the first ten wagons. In accordance with instructions from the Twelve, Anson's wagon train left the Missouri River for the West on July 22, 1846. Organized by priesthood authority, these Saints were directed toward the Rocky Mountains, and they went westward with great energy.

After traveling more than 130 miles through what is now Nebraska, this first wagon train was overtaken by new instructions, directing that it not proceed further that season. The wagon train found a place to winter, and then, in the spring of 1847, returned east and rejoined the main body of the Church on the Iowa side of the Missouri. There, Anson Call and his family remained for a year, making further preparations and helping others get ready for the trip west. It was two years after their initial start westward in 1846 that Anson Call and his family finally journeyed to the valleys of the mountains.[3] After his arrival, the obedient and resourceful Anson Call was frequently used by Brigham Young to begin new settlements in the Intermountain West.

What is the meaning of this pioneer experience? It is not enough that we are under call, or even that we are going in the right direction. The timing must be right, and if the timing is not right, our actions should be adjusted to the Lord's timetable.

The Lord's timing will be revealed through His servants. Several years ago President Gordon B. Hinckley announced the construction of a large number of new temples, essentially doubling the number of operating temples of the Church from about fifty to about one hundred in just a few years. Having additional temples has always been the direction to go, but until the prophet of the Lord signaled this as a major initiative, no one could have properly urged such a sudden and dramatic increase for the Church and its people. Only the Lord's prophet could move the whole Church west. Only the Lord's prophet could signal the Church to double its operating temples in just a few years.

We must also follow the Lord's timing with those we try to interest in hearing the gospel message. Proclaiming the gospel is His work, not ours, and therefore it must be done according to His timing, not ours. There are nations in the world today that must hear the gospel before the Lord will come again. We know this, but we cannot force it. We must wait upon the Lord's timing. He will tell us, and He will open the doors or bring down the walls when the time is right. We should pray for the Lord's help and directions so that we can be instruments in His hands to proclaim the gospel to nations and persons who are now ready—persons He would have us help today.

The Lord loves all His children, and He desires that all have the fulness of His truth and the abundance of His blessings. He knows when groups or individuals are ready, and He wants us to hear and heed His timetable for sharing His gospel with them.[4]

The Agency of Others

The achievement of some important goals in our lives is subject to more than the timing of the Lord. Some personal achievements are also subject to the agency of others. This is particularly evident in two matters of special importance to young people—missionary baptisms and marriage.

When Sister Oaks and I were in Manaus, Brazil, in 2001, I spoke to about a hundred missionaries in that great city on the Amazon. As I stood to speak, I was prompted to put aside some notes I usually use on such occasions and substitute some thoughts on the importance of timing—some of the scriptures and principles I have been talking about today.

I reminded the missionaries that some of our most important plans cannot be brought to pass without the agency and actions of others. A missionary cannot baptize five persons this month without the agency and action of five other persons. A missionary can plan and work and do all within his or her power, but the desired result will depend upon the additional agency and action of others. Consequently a missionary's goals ought to be based upon the missionary's personal agency and action, not upon the agency or action of others.

Applications to Our Lives

Someone has said that life is what happens to us while we are making other plans. Because of things over which we have no control, we cannot plan and bring to pass everything we desire in our lives. Many important things will occur in our lives that we have not planned, and not all of them will be welcome. The tragic events of September 11, 2001, and their revolutionary consequences provide an obvious example. Even our most righteous desires may elude us or come in different ways or at different times than we have planned.

For example, we cannot be sure that we will marry as soon as we desire. A marriage that is timely in our view may be our blessing or it may not. My wife, Kristen, is an example. She did not marry until many years after her mission and her graduation.

The timing of marriage is perhaps the best example of an extremely important event in our lives that is almost impossible to plan. Like other important mortal events that depend on the agency of others or the will and timing of the Lord, marriage cannot be anticipated or planned with certainty. Latter-day Saints can and should work for and pray for their righteous desires, but despite their efforts, many will remain single well beyond their desired time for marriage.

So what should be done in the meantime? Faith in the Lord Jesus Christ prepares us for whatever life brings. Faith in Christ prepares us to deal with life's opportunities—to take advantage of those we receive and to persist through the disappointment of those we lose. In the exercise of that faith we should commit ourselves to the priorities and standards we will follow on matters we do not control, and we should persist faithfully in those commitments whatever happens to us because of the agency of others or the timing of the Lord. When we do this, we will have a constancy in our lives that will give us direction and peace. Whatever the circumstances beyond our control, our commitments and standards can be constant.

Sometimes our commitments will surface at unexpected times and be applied in unexpected circumstances. Sometimes the principles we have taught to others come back to guide our own actions when we think we do not need them anymore. A personal experience illustrates this reality.

Most Latter-day Saint parents know the importance of giving their children reminders as they go out on a date. I did this with our children, and I think they heeded my counsel. During the time I was getting acquainted with Kristen, when I left the house to meet her, one of my children said to me with a twinkle in the eye, "Now, Dad, remember who you are!"

The commitments and service of adult singles can anchor them through the difficult years of waiting for the right time and the right person. Their commitments and service can also inspire and strengthen others. The poet John Greenleaf Whittier wrote of this in his wonderful poem "Snow-Bound," which contains this description of a dear aunt who never married:

> The sweetest woman ever Fate
> Perverse denied a household mate,
> Who, lonely, homeless, not the less
> Found peace in love's unselfishness,
> And welcome whereso'er she went,
> A calm and gracious element.[5]

Wise are those who make this commitment: *I will put the Lord first in my life, and I will keep His commandments.* The performance of that commitment is within everyone's control. We can fulfill that commitment without regard to what others decide to do, and that commitment will anchor us no matter what timing the Lord directs for the most important events in our lives.

Do you see the difference between committing to what *you will do,* in contrast to trying to plan that you will be married by the time you graduate from college or that you will earn at least X amount of dollars on your first job?

If we have faith in God and if we are committed to the fundamentals of keeping His commandments and putting Him first in our lives, we do not need to plan every single event—even every important event—and we should not feel rejected or depressed if some things—even some very important things—do not happen at the time we had planned or hoped or prayed for them to happen.

Commit yourself to put the Lord first in your life, keep His commandments, and do what the Lord's servants ask you to do. Then your feet are on the pathway to eternal life. Then it does not matter whether you are called to be a bishop or a Relief Society president, whether you are married or single, or whether you die tomorrow. You do not know what will happen. Do your best and then trust in the Lord and His timing.

Life has some strange turns. Some of my personal experiences illustrate this. When I was a young man I thought I would serve a mission. I graduated from high school in June 1950. Thousands of miles away, one week after my high school graduation, a North Korean army crossed the 38th parallel, and our country was at war. I was seventeen years old, but as a member of the Utah National Guard I was soon under orders to prepare for mobilization and active service. Suddenly, for me and for many other young men of my generation, the full-time mission we had planned or assumed was not to be.

Another example occurred after I had completed my service as president of Brigham Young University. A few months later the governor of the state of Utah appointed me to a ten-year term on the state supreme court. I was then forty-eight years old. My wife, June, and I tried to plan the rest of our lives. We wanted to serve the full-time mission neither of us had been privileged to serve. We planned that I would serve twenty years on the state supreme court. Then, at the end of two ten-year terms, when I would be nearly sixty-nine years old, I would retire from the supreme court and we would submit our missionary papers and serve a mission as a couple.

I had my sixty-ninth birthday in the summer of 2001 and was vividly reminded of that important plan. If things had gone as we had planned, I would now be submitting papers to serve a mission with my wife June.

Four years after we made that plan I was called to the Quorum of the Twelve Apostles—something we never dreamed would happen. Realizing then that the Lord had different plans and different timing than we had assumed, I resigned as a justice of the supreme court. But this was not the end of the important differences. When I was sixty-six, June died of cancer. Two years later, I married Kristen McMain, the eternal companion who now stands at my side.

How fundamentally different my life is than I had sought to plan! My professional life has changed. My personal life has changed. But the commitment I made to the Lord—to put Him first in my life and to be ready for whatever He would have me do—has carried me through these changes of eternal importance.

Faith and trust in the Lord give us the strength to accept and persist, whatever happens in our lives. I did not know why I received a "no" answer to my prayers for the recovery of my wife of many years, but the Lord gave me a witness that this was His will, and He gave me the strength to accept it. Two years after her death, I met this wonderful woman who now is also my wife for eternity. And I know that this was also the will of the Lord.

Do not rely on planning every event of your life—even every important event. Stand ready to accept the Lord's planning and the agency of others in matters that inevitably affect you. Plan, of course, but fix your planning on personal commitments that will carry you through no matter what happens. Anchor your life to eternal principles, and act upon those principles whatever the circumstances and whatever the actions of others. Then you can await the Lord's timing and be sure of the outcome in eternity.

The most important principle of timing is to take the long view. Mortality is just a small slice of eternity, but how we conduct ourselves here—what we become by our actions and desires, confirmed by our covenants and the ordinances administered to us by proper authority—will shape our destiny for all eternity. As the prophet Amulek taught, "This life is the time for men to prepare to meet God" (Alma 34:32). That reality should help us take the long view—the timing of eternity. As President Charles W. Penrose declared at a general conference memorializing the death of President Joseph F. Smith:

"Why waste your time, your talents, your means, your influence in following something that will perish and pass away, when you could devote yourselves to a thing that will stand forever? For this Church and kingdom, to which you belong, will abide and continue in time, in eternity, while endless ages roll along, and you with it will become mightier and more powerful; while the things of this world will pass away and perish, and will not abide in nor after the resurrection, saith the Lord our God."[6]

I pray that each of us will hear and heed the word of the Lord on how to conduct ourselves in mortality and set our standards and make our commitments so that we can be in harmony and in tune with the timing of our Father in Heaven.

From an address delivered at Brigham Young University on January 29, 2002.

NOTES

1. *Even As I Am,* Salt Lake City: Deseret Book, 1982, 93.
2. "Plow in Hope," *Ensign,* May 2001, 59.
3. Anson Call, *The Journal of Anson Call,* Afton, Wyo.: Ethan L. Call and Christine Shaffer Call, 1987, 35–39.

4. Dallin H. Oaks, "Sharing the Gospel," *Ensign,* November 2001, 7–9.
5. "Snow-Bound: A Winter Idyl," in *Snow-Bound: Among the Hills: Songs of Labor: and Other Poems,* Boston: Houghton, Mifflin and Co., 1898, lines 352–57.
6. In Conference Report, June 1919, 37.

Index

31–32; abortion and, 32; importance of marriage in, 32–33; bearing and nurturing of children as essential part of, 33–35; and Millennium, 35

Powerful ideas: importance of teaching, 45–46, 51; unequal values of knowledge of, 46

Prayer: as powerful idea, 47–48; Spencer W. Kimball on, 48

"Private University Looks at Government Regulation, A," 157

R

Reason, vs. revelation, 133

Reed, Virginia, 50–51

Remembering Jesus Christ: as part of sacramental covenants, 87; and remembering family, friends, and associates dear to us, 88–89; as our Redeemer, 89; by serving and forgiving our fellow men, 90–91; by striving to assure that all receive baptism, 91; as means of understanding and enduring life's afflictions, 91–92; by loving and doing good to one another, 92; by seeking those who feel left out, 92–93; by loving neighbors as ourselves, 93–94

Repentance: Bruce R. McConkie on, 118; necessity of, 118; in Church discipline vs. laws of man, 118–19, 121; and confession under laws of man, 119; confession as essential feature of, 119–20; restitution as key ingredient of, 120; and restitution under laws of man, 120–21; suffering and, 121–24; as primary purpose of Church discipline, 125–26; experiencing change of life through, 126–27; and avoiding sin, 127–28; and experience with curious son, 128; and discouragement used by Satan,

128–30; as acceptance of God's love manifest in the Atonement, 130

Restitution: as essential ingredient of repentance, 120; as privilege, 120; under laws of man, 120–21

Resurrection: as powerful idea, 48; as pillar of our faith, 53; scriptural witnesses of Christ's, 53–55; literality and universality of, 55–56; Joseph Smith on, 56; vital position of, in plan of redemption, 56–57; as source of strength for facing mortality's challenges, 57; as incentive for keeping commandments, 57–58; as encouragement to fulfill family responsibilities, 58; and restoration, 58; as source of courage to face death, 58–59; temple building as demonstration of faith in, 59; apostolic declaration of, 59–60

Revelation: and reason, 133; definition of, 149; James E. Talmage on, 149; forms of, 149–50; Boyd K. Packer on, 150, 161; Lorenzo Snow and Harold B. Lee on, 150; experience with birth of sixth child, 151; and prophecy, 151; received by Joseph Smith in Liberty Jail, 151; experience signing document as Brigham Young University president, 154; experience with new stake center, 154; experience preparing legal casebook for publication, 154–55; Bruce R. McConkie on doing all we can before seeking, 155–56; experience assisting members of Quorum of the Twelve in selecting stake presidents, 156; experience speaking to national association of attorneys, 157; experience of Chasty Olsen Harris being told to remove children from riverbed, 158; experience of Wilford Woodruff being told to move carriage, 158; experience writing

T